NEW
LOVE

NEW LOVE

Dr. Frank and Mary Alice Minirth
Dr. Brian and Dr. Deborah Newman
Dr. Robert and Susan Hemfelt

A
JANET
THOMA
BOOK

THOMAS NELSON PUBLISHERS
NASHVILLE

Copyright © 1993 by Brian and Deborah Newman, Frank and Mary Alice Minirth, Robert and Susan Hemfelt

All rights reserved. Written permission must be secured from the publisher to use or reproduce any part of this book, except for brief quotations in critical reviews or articles.

Published in Nashville, Tennessee, by Thomas Nelson, Inc., and distributed in Canada by Lawson Falle, Ltd., Cambridge, Ontario.

Scripture quotations are from the NEW KING JAMES VERSION of the Bible. Copyright © 1979, 1980, 1982, Thomas Nelson, Inc., Publishers.

Library of Congress Cataloging-in-Publication Data
New love : the first passage of marriage / Brian and Deborah Newman . . . [et.al.].
*   p.   cm.*
"A Janet Thoma book"—T.p. verso.
ISBN 0-8407-3464-6 : $8.99
*   1. Marriage—United States. 2. Communication in marriage—United States. I. Newman, Brian. II. Newman, Deborah.*
HQ734.N525 1992
306.81′ 0973—dc20
*   92-21053*
*   CIP*

Printed in the United States of America
1 2 3 4 — 96 95 94 93

Contents

Acknowledgments

THE AUTHORS wish to thank the many people who helped make this book possible. Many thanks to Sandy Dengler and Catherine Walkinshaw whose writing talents brought the illustrations, thoughts, and notes from the authors to a consistent and readable form. We also thank Janet Thoma for the many hours she spent guiding, editing, and directing the completion of the manuscript. We recognize Susan Salmon for her editorial assistance and attention to the details that helped make the book complete. Last, we acknowledge our children: Rachel, Renee, Carrie, and Alicia Minirth; Rachel and Benjamin Newman; Katy, Kristin, and Robert Gray Hemfelt, for the special part they add to our passages through marriage.

Chapter 1

The Passages: What They Are, What They Do

C arl Warden hated to see a grown man cry, himself especially. But the tears ran freely down his cheeks now, as Beth Anne came down the aisle. Praise God, she was beautiful! Warm, clear, suntanned skin against the white gown; long golden hair like her grandmother's, tumbling in loose waves; that uncertain, innocent smile. She was as beautiful as Annie had been on her wedding day, almost as beautiful as Bess had looked. Beside him, Bess gripped his arm and squeezed.

His granddaughter getting married—how old does that make you feel? He glanced over at his daughter, Annie. The mother of the bride still had that look of I've-got-it-all-together that had made her such a source of pride to Bess and Carl all these years. She watched her daughter, dewy-eyed, as Beth Anne approached the altar.

Annie had outdone herself with this wedding. All the details, the special little touches, the attention to small things—they added up to perfection. Yes, that was Annie. Carl could feel assured Annie had done it all too. Rob provided for her well enough, but he never lifted a finger to help with anything like this. You couldn't call him lazy, but you couldn't call him a go-getter, either. In all the years Annie and Rob Howe had been together, Carl could never get a really good, warm feeling for his son-in-law.

The wedding went off without a hitch; again, that was Annie and her planning. She even had the limo drivers wearing identical neckties as the wedding party moved across town to the reception at the Northside Country Club.

Bess wagged her head as she crawled into their own limo. "Can you imagine this?" Carefully she lowered herself in the seat. "When we got married we didn't ride around in limos."

"Naw." Carl chuckled and settled in beside her. "But as I recall, our wedding vehicle cost more than this does."

She laughed out loud. "True. A city bus costs more!"

The reception, too, hummed along flawlessly, like a well-oiled machine. Carl enjoyed being a guest of honor at a fancy "do" like this—one of the fringe benefits of old age. He shook hands with more people in two hours than he'd met in the last three years. Among them was an old business associate, Louis Ajanian. Carl had never seen him quite this cheerful. Louie, a widower, had remarried recently, and he still looked in the throes of new love. Her name was Margaret.

Carl also met Julia Karris at last. Beth Anne had been talking about her good friend Julia for years. Beth had described Julia's woes with the ex-husband, the present husband, the kids. Too bad about all the problems. Julia was such a charming woman, graceful, dark-haired, and beautiful.

Julia grasped his hand firmly. "Beth Anne is just gorgeous! You must be so proud."

"As an understatement, that'll do," Carl smiled.

"She's so lucky." A wisp of sadness edged her voice. "My mom never attended my weddings—either one of them—let alone my grandparents."

While the string quartet tuned up, Carl sat under a parasol and thought about this whole business. There was Louie, as happy with his bride as a pup in a dog food factory. There was Julia Karris, unlucky at love twice over but still trying to make a match work. Here was Annie, who seemed to hide problems, if she had any; he bet she did. And Beth Anne, just starting out. . . . He looked across the pool at Bess. Too bad every man in the world couldn't marry a woman like Bess. It would sure solve a lot of troubles. Then the string quartet began a waltz, and Anne with her Alan led off.

Carl finally managed to draw Annie aside as the event wound down. He gave her a warm squeeze. "Perfect, end to end," he crowed to his daughter. "You even arranged for right weather." He led her to a little bench along the edge of the expanse of green lawn. "Bet you're going to be glad to relax, after all this."

Annie's face darkened. She tried to smile; no smile came. "Dad . . ." She took a deep breath, and her eyes skittered about everywhere, anywhere except her father's face. "This wedding kept me busy, you might say. But now . . . now I have . . . I don't have anything to do. It's just Rob and me in that house." She turned to him.

"Your marriage is solid, Sugar Anne. What are you saying?" Carl tried to read her face; all he saw was fear. "You always said you'd be glad when the last child moved out."

"It's . . ." She waved a hand in the air, trying to pluck words that would not come. "Our marriage has changed somehow, Dad. He's not the same person. Or maybe I'm not. We don't have anything in common, or . . . I'm not even sure I love him anymore. And now it's only me and him, me and something I don't think I want. What am I going to do, Dad?"

Everyone's marriage, like Annie's, changes with time. So often, the changes are not for the better.

Who's Sorry Now?

Our very nature throws into marriage certain clinkers that we do not recognize and cannot anticipate. Those clinkers are generated by our families of origin—by the way our relatives did things, said things, and hid things. Dr. Hemfelt likens them to time-release capsules. Things can be chugging along comfortably. Suddenly, with no warning, one of those time-release beads goes off. The union is not what it was, and something has gone dreadfully awry.

Yet these clinkers, and the other inevitable changes in a marriage, can be turned from bad to good once you recognize what they are. A marriage that appears dull and mundane can be made to sparkle. A hopeless situation can emerge into bright promise. A good union can be made better. It all depends upon finding and managing the sources of trouble, the clinkers and changes. We want to help you do that.

Couples who approach professionals in the Minirth-Meier Clinic never come in because everything is going well. Rather, they sense trouble. They feel unmet needs. Their symptoms, the surface clues to underlying problems, show up in our case files again and again, however unique they may seem to the couples experiencing them. Because no marriage is perfect, every couple weathers these problems to some extent. But when the problems loom too large to handle and threaten the union, trouble will follow.

Look over the following hints of trouble in light of your own family relationships. Do some of them mar your happiness right now?

Chronic Financial Distress

Why can't Harry get ahead? He doesn't overspend. His wife, while not frugal, is not extravagant, either. Yet his ship of finance wallows up to its gunwales in debt. By this stage in life, Harry ought to be a unit manager, if not a store manager, but he's still clerking and stocking shelves. Harry knows why he can't get ahead. He's had to change jobs five times in the last ten years because of unfeeling, incompetent bosses. One of his employers even sent him to the company shrink to talk to him about his attitude problem. *His* attitude!

Then his wife cajoled him into marriage counseling for unrelated reasons. After a year of counseling at the Minirth-Meier Clinic in Dallas, Texas, Harry is still in debt, but at least now the bill collectors don't call him at home and work every day. He's working things out. He says, "I went to a financial counselor long ago. But what I learned from him simply didn't work until my marriage smoothed out." He grimaces. "And I didn't even know it was wrinkled."

Not all financial distress points to marriage problems, of course. We do, however, consider chronic financial difficulties a factor to examine closely. We also look closely if a person experiences constant or recurring vocational failure. This often points to some individual psychological problem or anger in the marriage. Maybe the husband wants to be married, yet a part of him longs for someone to take care of him. He buries that desire, but he unconsciously sabotages job after job. That's a warning signal. The husband is saying, "Yes, I've told you I want to be a breadwinner, but part of me feels that someone needs to take care of me." The man may never have felt he was well taken care of in his childhood. Maybe he was the child who never got the attention he deserved. Now he and his wife will have to work through these issues before they can establish a good relationship.

In-law Problems and Involvement

A related financial clue we address is any monetary dependence of the married couple upon the in-laws.

"But they prepared for us with trusts and legacies!" the couple might protest.

Absolutely. And we're all in favor of it. Inheritances as frosting on the cake are marvelous. What we look for, rather, is the prospect that the couple *requires* that legacy in order to survive financially.

Far more telling is a situation wherein the in-laws provide financial or intense emotional support long beyond the wedding, after the couple should have cut the economic and emotional apron strings and become independent. When newlyweds are engaged in a multigenerational family business, this particular red flag marks a lot of gray areas, some wholesome and some not.

In fact, in-law problems in general suggest that unfinished business—uncompleted passages—lie in the background. And though we will discuss unfinished business in detail later, keep in mind for now this broad generalization: Severe in-law friction indicates a cross-generational problem that, if not resolved, will fester in the present generation and infect the next ones.

Family Imbalance and Stress

Jason and Jennifer fight every day. They wish they didn't because it upsets the kids, just as their parents' fights used to upset them. But they believe bitter fighting is the mark of any marriage and the only way to resolve differences. Because Jennifer is right in most disagreements, she makes sure the kids are lined up on her side of the fence. And they are on her side because Jason is unnecessarily strict with them. They naturally resent that, preferring Jennifer's more easygoing ways. The fighting, of course, has moved into the bedroom, and Jennifer hasn't enjoyed their sexual expression for months. Oh, sure, Jason comes over now and then, but it's not fun anymore.

In one fell swoop, Jason and Jennifer illustrate what we look for in family imbalances: chronic fighting, sexual dysfunction, factional alliances within the family ("them" against "us"), and problems with and about kids.

Emotional or Psychological Dysfunctions

Jocelyn, a former model, fought a chronic depression for three years. Her husband sympathized, but he couldn't really understand her attitude. After all, he wasn't depressed. Their marriage was fine, their economic situation stable, the in-laws a thousand miles away. Obviously, he pointed out, it was her problem. Only when he entered into counseling with her and changed some basic attitudes and behaviors did her problem disappear.

Any emotional or psychological difficulty in one marital partner will invariably influence, and be influenced by, the other partner. Always.

Other symptoms we look for are anxiety, chemical dependence and addictions, and driving compulsions such as extreme perfectionism, workaholism, spendaholism, and such. Threats of suicide obviously hoist huge red banners.

The Influence of the First Passage

"Many of the problems couples will face in later years," says Dr. Robert Hemfelt, "don't show up in premarital plans and expectations."

And let's face it: probably much of what the person planning marriage hears in premarital counseling doesn't sink in. The situation is somewhat like that which automakers face when they introduce a new model.

After the designers and engineers pore over the plans for a new car model, they build a prototype. Then a test driver takes it out on the course and simply drives, and drives, and drives. Time in the saddle, so to speak, will reveal the little design flaws that the engineers couldn't see on paper. Not just flaws, either. The driver can make suggestions for improving comfort, performance, the feel of the road, the pleasure that comes from driving a fine machine.

Similarly, time in the saddle will reveal the design flaws in a marriage, as well as possible improvements. In a healthy, growing marriage, the marital partners deal with these matters as they surface over time. But some problems and improvements can be spotted on paper, so to speak, before the marriage has progressed far at all, or has even begun. That's what this book is all about.

The symptoms of trouble we mentioned above will steal the sheer pleasure of marriage and are best scrubbed right in the beginning. But they are merely the surface fluff. Their presence in your marriage, and their presence in the couples we counsel, say that something far deeper is going on. In this book we want to plumb the depths and sources of problems, rather than bandage the surfaces. These depths, the inner workings of marriage, can be compared to the dynamics of a softball game, believe it or not, which are not all that different from the dynamics of marriage.

The Dynamics of Marriage

The city league softball player steps up to the plate, shoulders his bat, and watches intently. Here comes the pitch. . . .

"It's a solid hit into deep right field!" the announcer screams exuberantly. The ball is still airborne as the player rounds first. It drops into tall grass—*very* deep right field—and a portly fielder scurries after it. The player passes third, homeward bound.

Wait! He failed to touch second! As his team groans in unison, he runs back to stomp second base. What would have been a home run ends up only a double, all because the runner failed to clear second base satisfactorily. Marriage is like that. We call the bases "passages."

When Doctors Newman or Minirth or Hemfelt deal with the marital problems of couples in their counsel, they deal with three entities: the husband, the wife, and the marriage itself, as if the marriage were a living, breathing organism. We have found that if a marriage is not growing, it is dying, just as you would say for any living organism. When a marriage gets hung up in a passage, it ceases growing. Growth is, therefore, critical.

By definition, then, *passages are predictable and necessary stages, involving the physical, the emotional, and the spiritual.* Through them, partners journey toward the lifetime goal of growth as individuals and as a couple.

In our personal lives and in our professional practice, the six authors of this book have identified five distinct stages, passages through which marriage passes. The developmental stages through which a child passes from birth into adulthood are well known. Similarly, a marriage matures from developmental stage to stage—from passage to passage—according to the number of years it has existed. Remarriage may differ somewhat; because the partners have been married previously, they might telescope a passage into a briefer time or extend a passage beyond its normal life span.

The Passages of Marriage

Not counting courtship, which by definition is a passage of premarriage, we divide the lifetime of a married couple into five distinct units. Although some people hasten ahead of time into the next passage, or linger a little longer than average in one passage or another, in general, normal, healthy marriages follow pretty close to this outline. The passages are these:

- The First Passage—New Love: the first two years. Whether the couple is eighteen years old or eighty, they pass first through this dewy-eyed stage of idealized love. Persons who have been married previously may go through it a little faster than those married for the first time, but everyone tastes its heady joy.

- The Second Passage—Realistic Love: from the second anniversary through the tenth. Kids and career put the push on. About now, too, a heavy dose of reality sets in. This perfect partner is not so perfect after all. If this is Eden, why the thorns?

- The Third Passage—Steadfast Love: from the tenth anniversary through the twenty-fifth. Wrapped up in career, kids, and a host of extraneous, time-consuming activities, the couple find themselves fallen into a rut. Either they're mushing along fairly complacently or at each other's throats, but there's a predictability about the whole thing.

- The Fourth Passage—Renewing Love: from the twenty-fifth through the thirty-fifth anniversary. As the kids fledge and the career peaks out, the meaning and purpose of life alters forever. Now what?

- The Fifth Passage—Transcendent Love: beyond the thirty-fifth anniversary. What a history this couple has! The texture of the marriage changes as the couple enter retirement and watch youth fade forever.

As the marriage moves from one of these passages to another—from base to base toward home plate, if you will —it also moves through specific conditions common to the human race. Crisis and conflict, intimacy, forgiveness, children, and memories form some of them.

Each of the passages through which every married couple travel, like bases on a softball diamond, must be appropriately dealt with if the next one is to count. And the tasks that accompany these passages must be completed before the next tasks commence. By tasks we mean attitude changes one must make and jobs one must complete in order to maintain an intimate marital relationship.

Should a runner skip over a base, inadvertently or on

purpose, dire problems result. Should a runner get stuck on one base, the only way he can leave is by walking away scoreless. That's infinitely less satisfying than making it to home plate, for the aim of the game from the very beginning is to make it home.

Carl and Bess Warden, married forty-eight years, were making it home. As painful as eventual separation and death would be, the Wardens both would know the peace and satisfaction of being able to say, "We did it."

One of every two married couples will never know that satisfaction.

During their long life together, Carl and Bess Warden did not talk to marriage counselors or become involved in marriage therapy of any sort, though counsel might have helped them navigate the difficult passages more easily. Yet Carl and Bess did not simply muddle through. They worked diligently at their marriage, and to the very end enjoyed the fruits of a growing, timeless, abiding love.

You may be thinking, *But my marriage is so different; nobody has a husband like mine, or a wife like mine.*

Don't be so sure.

What If My Marriage Doesn't Fit the Pattern?

Remember the age-guessing booth at fairs and carnivals long past? A rather rough-looking man with a four-day stubble would offer to guess your age within three years. If he guessed, he won and you paid him. If he missed, you won and he paid you. And he almost always won. Why? Because age makes itself known in certain ways, and the trained eye can see those ways in every person.

A marriage also ages in certain ways regardless of the persons involved, regardless of the circumstances. The same patterns prevail even though yours may be a most unusual union. In fact, what is "normal"?

Mary Alice and Frank Minirth know their marriage could probably never be considered normal.

"When we married," Mary Alice explains, "we were both in school. Frank, in medical school, studied day and night. I had two years yet to complete my degree, so I was studying too. It wasn't a normal, start-a-family situation. My first job was as a teacher in inner-city Little Rock. Definitely not normal! Frank worked a twenty-five-hour day completing his internship. Then, getting a practice started —not normal. Possibly, there's no such thing as a normal marriage."

Your own situation may be less stressful than the Minirths' or more. You may be fishing off the Alaskan coast or working in a bank in Topeka. What's normal?

The passages themselves are the norm, the common denominators of any marriage. They are universal. They form the skeleton upon which problems and pleasures attach.

Each of the authors of this book is at a different passage: Brian and Debi Newman in the Second Passage, Robert and Susan Hemfelt just approaching the Third Passage, and Frank and Mary Alice Minirth in the Fourth. All six of us will give you our personal experiences and/or our professional insights. In addition to counseling couples and leading marriage enrichment seminars, psychotherapists Brian and Debi put their advanced degrees to work on the staff of the Minirth-Meier Clinic. Dr. Minirth, psychiatrist and a cofounder of the clinic, takes special interest in marriage and family dynamics. Dr. Robert Hemfelt, psychologist, is well known and respected as a leader in the study of codependency and multigenerational issues.

But what issues can a couple have when they're just beginning a life together? Starting with those "I do's" at the altar, they're writing on a blank slate, aren't they? Not at all. We'll show how the past can affect your future.

Moreover, as the marriage inexorably changes, so will the way a young couple deals with it. If you know chess or backgammon, you recognize that the strategy shifts as the game proceeds. Your goals at the beginning of play are not the same as those at the end. It's that way with marriage too. The original contract ceases to serve and must be rewritten. We'll discuss how to do that so your marriage will stay on a solid foundation.

This Book: The First Passage

This book deals with that first crucial passage, the initial two years of a marriage, and incorporates all the material on the First Passage that is covered in our hardcover *Passages of Marriage*. In addition, you will find material and details we simply had no room for when we were discussing the problems and opportunities a lifelong marriage offers. We shall look at premarriage and the opportunities and perils of courtship. If your first marriage ended in divorce, it is important for your future happiness that you see the underlying reasons why it failed. We may be able to help with that. At the bottom of most divorces, trouble came when one or both partners got hung up in a passage and failed to complete its tasks.

We'll suggest ways to avoid fruitless friction and damaging conflict, and even how to turn conflict into a positive experience. Then, we will look at the tremendous payoff a good marriage returns when you treat it right from the very first day. A marriage, however, begins long before the wedding day. Let's look at the first stage—meeting, getting-to-know-you, courtship.

Chapter 2

Courtship Remembered: Looking Back at Your First Fragile Steps in the Journey of Love

*V*oodoo music, eerie and mysterious, drifted across the driveway from that apartment building to this one. Closing the window was out of the question; this late-spring evening in Houston was too sultry, too muggy. It didn't help that Susan was studying assiduously for her Abnormal Psychology exam tomorrow morning. It made the spooky music all the spookier. To be honest, call her work "cramming." She probably should have been a little more diligent about studying during the semester.

Still, the weird bearded guy across the way shouldn't be playing that stuff so loudly while he loafed in the apartment complex hot tub. Too reticent to go over and complain in person, she called security.

Susan Hemfelt laughs and her eyes sparkle.

"Robert and I lived in the same apartment complex for approximately three years before we were actually introduced. I was rather skeptical of fraternizing with any males living in the complex without knowing someone else that could provide a sort of 'background check' on the prospect. So, needless to say, friendly I was not.

"One evening a female friend from college—she lived in

the next building—suggested that we sit in the hot tub and 'discuss our disgust' with the dwindling acceptable male population. We had no sooner settled ourselves comfortably alone in the hot tub when we were invaded by two males.

"They obviously had a different agenda in mind—that is, to break the ice with us, so to speak. The harder they tried, the harder we tried—to ignore them. Of course we eventually gave in to at least informal introductions. We visited briefly before my friend and I went elsewhere. We were determined not to let them weaken our will to stay put-out with their gender. I would never *ever* have guessed that I had just met the man I would marry.

"Within a day or two of the meeting in the hot tub came a knock at my door. Not able to see who it was, I quizzed the caller through the door as to his intentions. Reluctantly and not sure exactly which neighbor he was, I opened the door to find the guy with the weird music, the hot-tub conversationalist—alias Robert Hemfelt. He asked me for a date. I said I'd have to think about it. He bravely replied that he'd check back with me later that day. I accepted upon hearing that we would get together with another couple.

"The evening was fun, but before I knew it he was telling the story of how someone had called security on him one night and complained about his music. I felt myself glow red and started to shift in my seat. He caught my crawl-under-a-rock expression and read it accurately.

" 'You were the one who called?' he asked.

" 'Yeah, well, what can I say? I didn't know your name. But I noticed the security guard knew exactly whom I was referring to when I described the music coming from your area.'

" 'That "voodoo" music, as he said you called it, was religious music, Gregorian and Augustinian chants.' "

Control in Courtship

Susan's tales about meeting the bearded lover of Gregorian and Augustinian chants reflect important aspects of the
meeting-and-courtship process. (Incidentally, Robert
Hemfelt, now clean-shaven, still enjoys sacred Christian
music including monastic chants.) The major issue, as it is
with any two human beings coming together, concerns
control and even more complex challenges as well.

Boundary Control

"Love at first sight? It was a rocky beginning." Susan
laughs, then sobers. "Perhaps the most critical point here is
that of control: We can and should begin to set boundaries
from the start in courtship."

Boundaries are the invisible lines that separate a person
from all other human beings. They are somewhat like the
fences in rural areas. Consider, for example, the farm country around Lancaster, Pennsylvania. Virtually all the fields,
whether tilled or pasture, are surrounded by fences. Even
most of the wooded lots are encompassed by fences. On
each farm, amid the fields and therefore amid the fences,
stand the house and barns and other outbuildings. Fields
along the road may be subdivided into homesites of a few
acres each. Some of those homes have fences to keep children from wandering. Some may have fences to keep the
neighbors' dogs out. Occasionally, hedges rather than
fences separate one property from another.

In all this countryside, no matter what the size of the
individual farm or home, five-acre lot and five-hundred-
acre farm are defined by a fence or hedge. But those
boundaries are physical, concrete.

Another form of boundary: "This is my property. That is
yours. Your cows graze on your land and I'll grow dahlias
on my land. Please keep your dog out of my yard and I'll
keep my kids out of yours." These stated boundaries are

not physical; they are abstract, oral contracts. But they are boundaries all the same. Lines have been drawn.

Susan maintained both concrete and abstract boundaries. Spontaneity—acting on whim—is fine if you're planning a relaxing day off or choosing from options on a luncheon menu. When dealing with an unknown other person, Susan did not act spontaneously. She proceeded with caution. Partly, of course, this was for safety's sake. A woman alone these days has cause to question who is knocking at her door. She asked before opening the door. She maintained a physical boundary—the room and the door itself—until she knew with whom she was dealing.

But she protected her boundaries in abstract ways as well. He asked; she considered. She retained and used the power of choice. She acquiesced when she knew they would be accompanied by others. Had he insisted or attempted to force his company, he would have been invading her boundary, just as if he were to invade physically by forcing the door and attempting to enter uninvited.

She knew from the start where the lines were drawn, where the fences ought to be. And she maintained them.

Susan maintained another sort of boundary as well. The policies she decided upon before she was called to apply them also constituted a healthy boundary. For example, her policy was, go double on the first date. A young woman may decide that the first date is dutch—each person pays his and her own way so that no one is indebted to the other. If she is wise, she knows before she leaves her door just how far, if at all, a physical relationship will progress.

All this applies equally to the man. He sets his boundaries, his priorities, his policies just as a woman.

All these boundaries are predicated upon the most important one. If you were to draw a circle to represent Susan at that time of her life, you would, symbolically, draw a firm line. She had, in other words, a firm idea of who she was and a firm resolve to maintain her fences and policies. A person with little sense of self, or with a flawed view of self or very low personal esteem, would appear as a faint circle, a fine line, perhaps even a broken line. A distant, unemotional, or rigid person (a polite way of saying "thick as a dock piling") would be drawn as a circle with an extraordinarily heavy line. Neither very thin nor very thick personal boundaries serve well. Both lead to problems.

Power Control

"Robert and I have never liked the same music," Susan confides. "We've worked around the issue as needed. We included both a classical string ensemble and a pop music band for our wedding reception. I listen to my music by myself in the car or when he is not home. He listens to his out by our hot tub and in his car. This was probably our first control issue. Next came the choice of which movie to see. We're still working on that one."

Control—who's the boss? Whenever two human beings come together, control will without fail become an issue. Control is so important we will deal with it at length later. But even in courtship and the first year of marriage, with the glow of new love blinding the lovers and causing a snicker from the friends, control issues come up.

"Usually, in the initial stages of a relationship," says Dr. Newman, "the couple will put disputes aside. They're both on their best behavior, you might say, and a dispute would suggest that they're not perfectly matched. Robert and Susan reached a very nice compromise with their wedding music. Each gave a little, in two senses of the word; each gave in somewhat, and each gave the other what he and she preferred."

Giving is actually pretty easy early in a relationship. Each desires eagerly to please the other, to make points. Withholding can be harder. *Will I damage my relationship by being stubborn or selfish? Can I cause a rift that separates us before we ever get started?*

Susan assumed the risks, confident that controlling her boundaries was an important long-term commitment. But she kept the imaginary line defining herself flexible enough to give on nonessential issues (nobody's going to live or die on the basis of what music shows up at the wedding). Her groom felt the same way. Had Robert not—had he remained adamant about his classical music—she could choose to either hang tough herself, give in as a love gift to Robert and to the occasion, or set off with him in pursuit of some style of music agreeable to them both.

All this is extremely hard for a new couple to work out, for as much as they imagine they know each other's inner-most feelings and desires, they are barely acquaintances at this stage of their relationship. They know nothing of the depths.

Underlying boundary issues and control issues are deeper issues. These present difficult challenges which the new couple must master if the relationship is to grow.

Challenges in Courtship

"I call prepassage—that is, premarriage—courtship the time of great illusion," says Dr. Hemfelt. "The couple nurtures this fond illusion of oneness. Sameness. Getting past the illusion isn't a task, exactly. Call it a challenge."

The First Challenge: To See Through the Illusion

Here is the great task of courtship: See through the wonderful, beautiful, crippling illusion of oneness. Chip through to a view of the real person. Mary and Hank illustrate the concept.

"We fit together like hand and glove," crowed Mary at her quitting-the-job office party.

"Yeah," mumbled Hank, her fiancé. "A boxing glove."

Hank's balloon of illusion had been punctured. Mary's, as yet, had not. Hank was actually in a better position to grow, for he could see reality in clearer light.

"She drives me nuts," Hank complained. "She's always twenty minutes late. Always."

"When did you first notice?" his friend Walt asked.

"Just recently, I guess. Couple months."

"How long have you two been going together?"

Hank counted mentally. "A year, about."

"What made her change now?"

Hank thought about that a minute. "Well, I guess she didn't change. She's always been that way. I just didn't notice it before."

Hank had stumbled upon one of the barriers to breaking the illusion: selective perception.

Selective Perception

Persons just commencing a relationship want desperately to be matching up with the perfect partner. As a result, they see only what they want and literally blind themselves to annoyances and flaws. What is either dismissed or ignored now, of course, will become a sore spot later and a constant source of aggravation.

Perhaps the girl fails to notice he drinks. Or she may see he drinks but unconsciously chooses not to see how much. Selective perception.

A man or woman sees signs of abusive behavior in the new partner and dismisses them. Surely that abusive behavior is merely a reaction of wild passion. The eye sees; the heart ignores.

In clinical situations, counselors are tipped off to serious problems of selective perception when descriptions fail to match reality. For example, the therapist may ask, "And what is your fiancée like? Describe her." The gentleman describes her in glowing terms. Then the lady comes in for the first time, and the counselor is downright startled because she is not in the least the way her beloved described her. His description bears little relationship to a detached view.

Selective perception diminishes with time. Well-meaning friends may try to speed it up (particularly if they don't much approve of the match) by pointing out faults, flaws, and differences. But the real change in perception must come from within; the heart must see. And that comes, usually, with time. As the problem of perception fades with time, another barrier emerges—the deferred resolution of differences.

Deferred Resolution of Differences

In common five-cent words, this five-dollar phrase, deferred resolution of differences, means, "I'll change my spouse after we're married."

Mary used this to deal with Hank's penchant for army surplus clothes. Hank skulked through life clad in sloppy, faded, camouflage coveralls. He liked them. They felt comfortable. His idea of a black-tie affair was replacing the camouflage shoestrings in his boots with dark ones.

In premarital counseling, Mary declared, "He doesn't dress very well now, but once we're married I can turn that around. I can make him different."

I Can Make Him/Her Different.

Mary must come to realize, as must all courting and newly married couples, that what you see is pretty much what you get. Certainly people change as they grow. But rarely will the changes be the changes the couple envision beforehand.

As differences surface in courtship, they must be either resolved or accepted. The courting couple must yield to the bare, honest, painful truth: that the person is not going to change in order to fit into the other's preconceived mold.

Neither Hank nor Mary at this point had realized another crucial point. As a rule, all through courtship both partners are on good behavior, or at least semigood behavior. Mary drives Hank crazy with her twenty-minute tardiness. What neither of them realizes is that she is normally forty minutes behind. She's been trying to be better about punctuality, even if she doesn't consciously realize it.

Hank doesn't just like his camouflage wear, he has no idea what clothes are more appropriate. He was never taught dress sense by his parents, and the dress code at his high school was nonexistent. Guys slouched around in just about anything. He has no idea what constitutes "formal," "casual," "smart casual," or any other dress style.

This good behavior, then, makes the differences all the more frightening, for they run deeper than they seem. Sooner or later, both Hank and Mary will revert to their old ways, with dire consequences. They'll irritate each other more, disappoint each other more, argue more, feel greater friction.

And not know why.

Of course, Mary and Hank tried to discuss her tardiness and his dress a few times. But both felt a little uptight and defensive about the issues. Both decided, below conscious level, to talk about it some other time. Deferred.

"But wait," says the reader. "Things like that seem rather superficial."

And we agree. Almost always, though, superficial issues such as style of dress go hand in hand with deeper issues such as money or sexuality or spirituality. When we counsel couples we must, of course, get down to core issues, the deep fundamentals. To do so we begin with superficial, funny things, then dig deeper. Which side of the roll should the toilet paper emerge from, the front or the back? What's so wrong with twenty minutes late? Just give Mary a false time, half an hour earlier, and you'll be ten minutes early. Superficial differences are important because they open the gate to bigger issues.

The couple starting out, then, either fails to see differences or sees them and puts off their resolution. But there is still another barrier to climb.

Pursuit of the Ideal Person

"Mary and Hank provided a perfect illustration of this problem," Dr. Hemfelt related. "Both of them were pursuing an ideal in their mind's eye and not the actual person, not the way the other person really was."

For example, in premarital counseling, Mary described the perfect husband. He would graduate from college and go to work for a major corporation, relentlessly climbing the corporate ladder. That picture of success and security came pretty much as a result of her father's constant coaching over the years.

She picked a man, Hank, who was just finishing college. He had not graduated yet, had not so much as begun the job interview process.

When Dr. Hemfelt talked to her, she kept putting forth the ideal that Hank would finish college. She more than just knew it. She assumed it.

When Dr. Hemfelt talked to Hank privately, he learned that Hank's ideal was to quit college and start his own business. As Hank explained it, "When I talk with Mary, I talk about corporate jobs as a possibility, sure. But that's not the real me. That's not my dream. Ever wander through a stationery store? Office supplies? I mean, just wander and look?"

"Well, yes," Dr. Hemfelt allowed.

"They fascinate me. I love the orderliness, I guess, and the variety. And with the explosion in software and computer technology, they're expanding rapidly. It's not just pens and paper anymore. I want to provide the best and latest for customers who need specialized supplies as well as the standard stuff. I want my store to be the place to go. And I even know how I want to launch it."

Hank absolutely glowed as he articulated his dream.

Mary would not have recognized it as a dream. You see, she projected her dreams onto Hank and pretended they were his. Her ideal was what she hoped he would be or what he would adopt as his own. Sooner or later, reality would sucker-punch her with a knockdown blow.

On the other hand, Hank pictured himself marrying a stay-at-home helpmate. Mary happens to be a very bright young woman and plans to complete her education at least to the master's degree level. Hank talked only about his future homemaker. The problem here was not that the two roles are incompatible. The problem was that Hank could not hear what Mary was saying. "I plan to be a career person," she repeated over and over. The declaration ricocheted right off him. He was not dating the real Mary; he was dating his ideal.

Each couple must combat this illusion problem by asking, and answering, a most important question: "Am I dating the real person or am I dating a delusion?"

To answer that one you must listen to what your intended is actually saying, not to just what you want to hear.

Breaking through the illusion is only part of it. There is also the matter of why couples engage in a courtship in the first place.

The Second Challenge: Ferret Out the Reasons for Marrying

In the film *The Last Picture Show,* the characters portrayed by Cybil Shepherd and Jeff Bridges elope. As they rip down the highway, driving to Oklahoma, the man realizes that this girl is not eloping to marry him, she's eloping as an act of rebellion against her mom and dad. She manages to let her parents know her destination, the last thing you do if you're escaping.

In counsel we too frequently find that both courtship and marriage become not an act of love but leverage for leaving home. Persons who exploit courtship and marriage as a way to get out of the household of origin have not authentically left home on their own. A couple of years down the road, as they slip from Passage One into Passage Two, serious problems will surface. Count on it.

The question every person must answer: "Am I authentically leaving home on my own for myself, or am I using courtship, marriage, and this other person as a lever to pry loose from home?"

When Beth Anne announced her intention to marry Alan, her mother, Annie, popped the clutch and roared away down the bridal path, planning, planning, planning. Annie buried herself in plans and details. She was repeating a pattern she had used her whole marriage. Rather than face deep, tough questions, she inundated herself in little things. The tyranny of the immediate—that is, the necessity to take care of urgent little details—robbed her of the time she might have spent in careful introspection of deep issues.

Some of the tough questions facing her:

- "What will I do now that my daughter is leaving home?"
- "Is Alan a good choice? Can I bring myself to love him as I love Beth Anne?"
- "Am I prepared to shift roles from mother to mother-friend, and to accept my daughter's new role of no-longer-child-but-woman?"

Swamped to the gunwales in the elaborate preparations of a world-class wedding, Annie put those questions aside. Beth Anne should have been asking herself:

- "Am I marrying Alan to start a new life with a wonderful man, or is this simply a legitimate way to leave home, where I feel ignored?"
- "Am I marrying Alan because I love him or because I

want to manipulate a situation, for two of us, where I can seemingly get all the attention I crave?"

Fortunately, during premarital counseling, Beth Anne's pastor asked the two of them to write down reasons for getting married. "Brainstorm," he urged them. "Write down not just reasons you think apply to you personally, but any reason that anyone might have."

Beth Anne had a great time coming up with ridiculous reasons as well as the serious ones that applied to her.

"Now," her pastor suggested, "explain to yourself why each of these reasons applies to you."

"But they're off the wall!" she protested. "I did them for kicks. Goofing off. This one for instance: 'Maw and Paw don't like me chewing tobaccy around the house.' "

The pastor grinned. "I assume you don't smoke and you don't chew."

"And I don't kiss no boys what do." She completed the familiar couplet with a smile.

"So forget the tobacco part. What is the statement really saying?"

"But—"

"Really saying?"

Beth studied her paper a moment. "It's saying I don't like it around home, and I'm eager to start another home with different rules." She looked up. "Is that what you mean?"

"Even more important, that's exactly what *you* mean."

Beth Anne, neglected her whole life because Mom was always busy with some project, wanted a new home with new rules.

How About You?

Make a list of all the reasons in the world why anyone would get married. (Let your mind roam free, as Beth Anne did, when she listed, "Maw and Paw don't like me chewing tobaccy.")

1. _____
2. _____
3. _____
4. _____
5. _____
6. _____
7. _____
8. _____
9. _____
10. _____

Now take a second look at those reasons. Could any of them, or their underlying meanings, apply to you? What insights can you glean from your heart's off-the-wall mind games? (Consider each of those ten reasons individually, as Beth Anne did when she said, "It's saying I don't like it around home, and I'm eager to start another home with different rules.") Fill in the following blanks with an insight for each of the off-the-wall reasons you gave above.

1. _____
2. _____
3. _____
4. _____
5. _____
6. _____
7. _____
8. _____
9. _____
10. _____

Making Peace with the Wrong Reasons

Marrying for all the wrong reasons is not a guarantee that the marriage will fail. It doesn't even mean certain unhappiness. A lot of people who married wrongly discover it wasn't such a bad decision after all. However, knowing your motives beforehand eliminates a lot of problems ahead of time, and one small problem ironed out before the fact is ten problems avoided later on. Every marriage needs all the help it can get. Any steps you take to understand yourself and your relationships during courtship will pay big dividends in the future.

If you sense that you are having trouble growing out of your family of origin in a healthy way, we recommend sources such as *Love Is a Choice,* with which you can explore your family relationships and see if there is room for improvement.

Beth Anne had to grieve, to heal, to make peace with the realities of her childhood and her courtship. Once she did that and said good-bye to her parents' home, she could step out with confidence, marrying Alan for all the right reasons.

"Like, he claims he makes the world's best ranch breakfast," Beth Anne giggled. "I can't wait to sleep in one Saturday morning and let him do the cooking."

And so Beth Anne and Alan came together in matrimony, for good reasons and for not-so-good ones. The important thing for their future is they discussed their reasons together, bravely laying bare their inner feelings. It was a pattern that would serve them well for a lifetime.

But there are some other steps they could take in the beginning that would serve them well later. One of these is to start a trove of shared memories.

Thanks for the Memories

Why, Carl Warren mused to himself, *did they pick this place? Oh, well. They did.* He sat in a Naugahyde-upholstered booth in La Tapatia, the best Mexican restaurant in town. Mariachi music blared a little too loudly through the overhead speaker. Orchids, hibiscus, and huge, gaudy macaws were painted here and there on the stucco walls. Macaws graced the paper placemats. Even the sugar packets were imprinted with the restaurant logo, a scarlet and blue macaw.

Beside him, Bess finished up her favorite Mexican dinner, the chili relleno and enchilada combo plate. Across from them sat Beth Anne and Alan, obviously enjoying the food and the atmosphere.

Carl put his question into words. "When Bess and I invited our granddaughter and her best beloved out for a special dinner, we thought you'd pick a fancy place. You know, tassles on the menus, snooty waiters, mint-flavored toothpicks."

Alan grinned self-consciously. "We talked about it. That restaurant in the Regency, for instance, with the velvet wallpaper. But then, we asked ourselves, 'Do we want ritzy for the sake of ritzy, or do we want comfort and pleasure?' We're both really comfortable in this place. We like it a lot, and the food's great. No contest."

Carl nodded. "Don't know if I ever mentioned it, but you two kids make us proud. You stop and think and make mature decisions."

Beth Anne burst out in a messy spate of giggles. She tried to muffle them in her napkin.

"What's so funny?" Carl looked from face to face.

"You wouldn't call us 'mature' if you knew some of the weird stuff we did. Goofy stuff normal people don't do when they're courting."

"Oh, I don't know." Through Carl's memories raced some truly strange incidents he and Bess had experienced long, long ago. "Such as?"

Beth Anne leaned forward a little. "Such as, we climbed up into a construction project, a new building on our college campus. We laid boards out and made it to the second floor ledge of the adjacent building. Then we soaped the windows of Alan's major professor's office. Oh, we didn't use soap. We used moist scouring powder, so it would hose off quickly and not leave any traces. We didn't want to be cruel. Then we made it back to the construction, pulled in the boards, and no one ever guessed who did it or how."

"Not as goofy as Aubray and Joyce," Alan added. "They lived in the Happy Trails trailer park, he in C and she in M. They pulled practical jokes on each other. One day Aubray's trailer started stinking, like something *big* died. He knew Joyce was the culprit, but he couldn't find out what she did. He searched for days and slept outside under a cottonwood tree in his sleeping bag. He married her five weeks early just so he could move into her trailer."

"I think that was her reason all along," Beth Anne smirked.

Alan continued, "Months later, the trailer park manager went up on the roof of C to service the air conditioner. He found the mummified remains of a two-foot-long carp Joyce had tossed up there, right by the intake."

And Now, You . . .

One of the pleasures of marriage, especially in later years, is shared memories. They mean more and more as time rolls on. Too, those memories will help ease the way through rough times, for they forge a strong bond between man and woman.

"Remember when we . . . ?"

"Remember how we . . . ?"

"We weathered some rough times together. We can hang in with each other this time."

Now, at the very beginning and even during courtship, is the time to commence a store of memories. Use scrapbooks, journals, videotape, a shoebox—perhaps all of them—to gather mementoes and notes. Don't assume, "My dear, we will always remember this moment."

You probably won't.

Beth Anne and Alan wrote down not only the window incident but their friends' carp caper as well. They journaled the events and incidents that delighted them, that gave them pleasure, that offered mutual insight. As they went along, they didn't collect big things or expensive things.

And they documented everything. They left none of their memories to memory. Attached to a little umbrella from Beth Anne's bridal shower was a note explaining where it came from and giving the date.

"I so wish I'd done that," Bess Warden sighed when she heard about Beth Anne and Alan's incipient memory trove. "Think of all we'd have now, after nearly fifty years!"

"Never too late to start." With a smug grin, Carl pocketed an empty sugar packet with a scarlet and blue macaw.

Into the First Passage

In the blur of a breathless moment, the wedding day comes and goes. The deed is done. The new life commences. As courtship provided the foundation for this initial union, so the First Passage forms the foundation of a lifetime commitment.

Now we will explore the tasks that must be completed if this First Passage is to be satisfactorily completed.

Chapter 3

Can Two Independent Persons Become One Unit?

Y ou've seen it in encyclopedias, if not in actual use. It looks like a kind of walking stick, something a proper gentleman would take out on a stroll through the park. When the gentleman wishes to sit down, he unfolds the top of his walking stick into a seat of sorts and there perches, his weight on the single-legged stool and both heels firmly pressed into the ground. It looks dreadfully uncomfortable, but actually, it's not bad.

Geometry buffs understand why a stool sits best on three legs; three points define a plane. They also define a stable marriage. A four-legged stool will wobble if all four legs are not exactly even and sitting on a flat surface. A one- or two-legged stool cannot stand alone. But you can perch a three-legged stool on uneven ground and sit securely. You can tip a three-legged stool forward while you're milking, the better to manage a bored cow who's finished eating. A three-legged stool adapts solidly to any situation.

Every marriage exists as a three-legged stool. One leg is the husband; another is the wife. The third leg changes through time; it might be the kids or the job or buying and furnishing a home or, as in Annie Warden Millen's case, arranging a perfect wedding. That third leg always gets kicked out. The kids leave home. Retirement ends the job. Annie's daughter's wedding became history. Suddenly the stool's remaining two legs only have each other. That prospect terrified Annie, you remember, as it does many middle-aged couples.

"I remember," one of our clients recalled, "the night before our youngest child went to college. I sat on the sofa looking across the room at my husband in his recliner, and I thought to myself, *What in heaven's name will we ever talk about when the kids are gone? Do we have anything in common besides them?*

In this beginning passage of marriage, the stool is only two-legged and therefore unstable. The happy newlyweds are certain that in each other their lives are complete. They don't think they need a third leg. Their lives don't have room for one. As a result, the marriage bond at first is extremely fragile and easily hurt, as are the marriage partners.

The First Task: To Mold into One Family

The first task newlyweds must accomplish if they are to complete the First Passage—to mold two absolutely different, independent persons into one unit while preserving the individuality of both partners—won't come easily. It didn't come easily for Carl and Bess Warden two generations ago or for Annie and Rob. Beth Anne and Alan will also find some rough sledding.

Unity vs. Individuality

A couple of days after Beth Anne and Alan returned from their honeymoon, they came over to Bess and Carl Warden's to pick up some spare furniture.

Carl and Alan talked a while of occupations and former

occupations. "I don't know," Alan said, "if Beth Anne ever mentioned I used to break horses."

"Nope." Carl Warden smiled. "But I figured there had to be some reason you wore boots to your reception."

"I was gonna wear them to the wedding, but Annie blew the whistle."

"I'd guess breaking horses is pretty rewarding," Carl mused. "You're doing something productive, and no two situations are alike. So you have to be creative in how you deal with them."

"That's it exactly. The easiest job is to take a two-year-old filly or colt and teach it the bare essentials. Then you hand it over, green broke, to a professional trainer who teaches it a specialty, like barrel racing, cutting, or maybe just pleasure riding. I do that myself sometimes, but it takes a lot of work."

"What's the hardest job?"

"Breaking a team to harness." Alan sipped lemonade. His voice told Carl that here was his first love—after Beth Anne, of course. "Now take your average Belgian or Shire. Each horse weighs about an even ton. Tie two of 'em close together. Two tons of horse wouldn't be so bad if it wasn't operated by two separate brains. Horses have personalities and likes and dislikes just the same as people. If you get two horses that don't particularly like each other, or two horses that think along different lines, it takes about half of forever to work them into a well-matched team. And you never do get two that think alike."

Carl nodded sagely. "You know, Alan, you're talking as much about marriage as teams of horses."

Take two headstrong individuals and forge them into a unit without sacrificing their individuality. What a formidable task! To get through the First Passage of New Love with flying colors, you, as well as every other newlywed, have to master this task. Several things help in completing it.

On the Plus Side

A powerful tool comes built into this task of New Love: excitement and enthusiasm—raw, exuberant energy. Louis Ajanian married Margaret Holtz late in life. Louie is fifty-eight and Marj fifty-four. Louie, widowed three years before he met Marj, was a veteran of thirty-four years of marriage. Because Marj's first husband deserted her eight years into their union, she developed a strongly independent personality. She had to, with four kids to raise. Regarding their attitudes toward marriage, Louie and Marj are poles apart. And yet, both are just as excited about their new union as are Beth Anne and Alan.

On the Other Hand

One thing seriously hinders the move to unity: the possibility of breakage.

"Breakage?" exclaims the new couple. "What could break? We're young and indestructible and in love."

Regardless of what the couple think (or imagine), their intimacy in the beginning is superficial. True intimacy grows only as a couple get to know each other better. Persons in a new relationship have not had enough chronological time to do that in depth. This is true no matter what the actual age of the persons involved. Teenagers and seventy-year-olds suffer equally. They feel compelled to walk on eggs, as it were, when dealing with each other. "Will this upset her?" "How will I tell him about _____ ?"

Alan explained this about breaking a team of horses to harness: "The only way you get a horse team used to being driven together is by harnessing them up and working them. A large part of training is just getting out and driving them." A new couple, regardless of chronological age, has simply not logged enough time in harness to develop deep intimacy. Unfortunately, many marriages end in these first years, during this tenuous period.

Often a new couple inadvertently strain their fragile inti-

macy by loading it with burdens it cannot carry. "This is
the intimate relationship that will solve all my other relationship problems from the past. I will finally receive what
I need." Friction with parents, failed prior relationships,
perhaps even failed marriage—all melt away in the brilliant
heat of this new and encompassing love.

Julia Karris, Beth Anne's friend who was so unlucky in
love, unconsciously put that kind of weight on her marriage to Jerry Karris. She told us, "Rick Astin, my first
husband, is a charmer. Oh, what a charmer! He's really
good-looking. In fact, Greg is going to grow up looking a
lot like him. Rick has this mellow baritone voice that could
coax the shell off a coconut. So persuasive. And he's got a
bottomless supply of self-confidence. He tells you something and you just know he's going to deliver. He doesn't,
but he's such a con artist you don't realize he's ripping you
off."

"Ripping you off?" we asked. "You mean emotionally?"

"Emotionally, financially, every which way. He takes. He
soaks up. And he goes out looking for more. He never
gives."

"And you married Jerry because he's a giver."

"Yeah. After all those empty years with Rick, I deserve to
get a little back."

We learned also that Julia's parents, wrapped tightly in
their respective career ambitions, had each assumed the
other was providing Julia's nurturing. She could not remember a single instance when she sat on a parent's lap to
have a story read. She does, however, remember her children's book-plus-cassette tape sets, nearly a hundred of
them. Her tiny little tape player read to her as she turned
the pages. By talking about her childhood extensively, we
led Julia to see that here was another love hunger, another
lack, she was expecting Jerry to fill. The past is much too
onerous a burden for one relationship to endure, so the

couple must deal with some of those time-release capsules Dr. Hemfelt mentioned in Chapter 1.

What Are Time-Release Capsules?

Alan stared morosely at his glass of orange juice. He studied his cold capsule, one of those pills with all the little time-release beads inside. "Orange juice is acid, right?"

Carl looked at him across the table. "Right."

"So what if the acid pops all those time-release thingies in my stomach at once?"

"Don't worry about it. You eat Bess's chili, don't you?"

Time-release capsules as Dr. Hemfelt defines them are those quirks and unresolved issues in the parents' marriage —yes, and the grandparents', too, that we unknowingly carry into our new adult unions. They rarely explode at once. They pop in unexpectedly and usually go unrecognized. They might be benign; they might be very damaging.

Alan's mom and dad were volatile fighters, and he vowed never to be that way. His dad yelled. His mom cut, with clever and scathing remarks. Alan never thought about his parents' style of arguing. And he made sure he never yelled. He didn't realize, though, how much he hurt Beth Anne when he lashed back with some nasty, witty little response.

Alan did not know, either, that during their courtship, his parents never fought. On their best behavior, they reasoned things through with smiles and hugs. Alan and Beth Anne did a lot of smiling and hugging, before the ceremony. The cutting remarks were a time capsule, set to remain latent until the marriage was launched and rolling.

The use of cute remarks and funny lines that uplifted and did not hurt would have been a benign time capsule, a family pattern worth perpetuating and not damaging.

Can you see how this capsule could be very damaging? Or, how it could be harmless depending upon its release?

Throughout the rest of this book, we will refer to these time-release capsules and the influence they can have on your marriage. They are born from your family-of-origin patterns.

Putting Some Family Patterns Behind

Pulling up roots exists in many dimensions. The bride and groom have successfully left home. They're on their own. But the home has not left them.

The old patterns from home color nearly everything in the new marriage. Do you open gifts on Christmas Eve or Christmas morning? Do you make your bed immediately upon rising or when you go through the house tidying up? Which is right? The way you did it when you were growing up is right, of course. Any other way, though not exactly wrong, isn't right, either.

Obvious examples such as those above seem overly simplistic, but far more subtle "rights" and "not rights" color our day-to-day. What's more damaging, they color a mate's perception of the spouse. We find in counsel that "what's right" often forms the basis of habits the mate considers annoying:

- "Her table manners are atrocious. Elbows on the table, using her knife with her left hand. . . ."
- "He leaves the cap off the toothpaste tube. That drives me right out of my tree."

To these complaints the mate usually responds, "What's the big deal? You'd think I was robbing a bank!"

What About You?

Can you see the subtle traps? More importantly, do you see this sort of thing in your own marriage (or, if you are divorced, your former marriage)? How much of your mate's petty annoyances are founded on the way you were raised? The question is worth considering in depth and at leisure. You can "cure" a mate's annoying habits by either changing the habits or changing your annoyance. Identifying the source of the annoyance often ameliorates it.

Just knowing about annoyances may not be enough. You have to decide if it is worth making an issue of them. And you have those family-origin triggers to make matters worse.

Debi Newman recalls a rocky bump in her union with Brian.

"From an early age Brian did a lot of the cooking and grocery shopping. Even cleaning. He's very good at what you normally associate as a housewife's chores. In my house, Mom did most of that and she didn't need any help.

"When I was single, if lettuce was on the grocery list, I'd grab a head of lettuce. They all looked alike to me. After we married, Brian and I would push the grocery cart down the aisle together, very romantic, shopping. I'd toss a head of lettuce into the basket. He'd take my choice out of the cart, put it back, and choose another.

"I found that terribly threatening. Brian, the husband, was better at a job that was traditionally supposed to be mine, and he knew it. He really did pick the best lettuce.

"It took me a long time to realize, and then to accept, that the roles tradition assigns to a marriage are nothing more than guidelines. My mom did all the shopping in our home. Brian's family of origin was much different, giving him a much different body of experience from mine. He was reflecting his background just as my attitudes reflected mine. It's healthy. We eat better lettuce. But it's also healthy in that we can appreciate each other's unique gifts better now. From that original bump to my ego has come increased intimacy."

One bad ideal to hold now is that my spouse must change in order for me to be happy. If my spouse loves me, that person will become what I want him or her to be. What is needed at this stage (as well as all other passages of marriage) is unconditional acceptance of our mates. They are who they are and we love them because of that.

Unconditional? Only one person is capable of extending true unconditional acceptance, and that is God Himself. To accept a human person unconditionally is an ideal, not a reality. It's impossible to earn approval with no reservations. There are too many little kinks in the psyche, too many flaws. We are fallen. And so we come as close as we can to true unconditional acceptance, and the closer we come, the happier we are.

The time-release capsules from our childhood can be more destructive than simple "do's and don'ts" of running a household. They can be issues that harmed your parents' marriages, and your grandparents' too, and can eventually harm yours. Such issues can invade major decisions, like financial matters.

The Money Pit

For example, who will handle the finances in the new family? Julia Karris talked about her first marriage. "My mom balanced the checkbook, paid the bills, all that stuff. Dad said if she was willing to, he didn't want to be bothered. She was good at it."

"Did it cause conflict?" we asked.

"Not really. They both preferred the arrangement. In Rick's family, his dad did all that. If his mom wanted to write a check, she had to ask for the checkbook and tell why she wanted it."

"And Rick wasn't about to give up the purse strings."

"You got it. In the first six months we overdrew the checking account five times, because we both carried checkbooks and never talked to each other before writing big checks. What a mess!"

Indeed, what a mess. Differing perspectives and lack of communication caused serious problems for Julia and her first husband. "This is how it's supposed to be done, because this is how a family always does it." Those perspectives came directly out of the family of origin. They always do.

Julia Karris correctly identified that her attitudes toward money came out of her family of origin, as did her first husband's and her present husband's—time-release capsules of the most invidious sort. You would probably agree that yours do also. But what to do about it?

We asked Julia to take a careful look at her parents' marriage through a series of inventories similar to the ones in *Getting Ready for Marriage*, a workbook written by Jerry Hardin and Dianne Sloan (Nashville: Thomas Nelson, 1991), to help couples lay the foundation for a happy, healthy marriage. Although this particular workbook is designed for couples contemplating marriage, the principles work well for use in marriage recovery and enrichment, especially during this initial New Love passage.

The workbook contains several categories of statements. One series reflects the couple's parents' attitudes and habits. Julia and her present husband, Jerry, answered a series of true-false questions. Each question had two spaces for answers: You answer according to your own gut feelings, and you also answer as you believe your mate would.

To the statement, "I think credit card balances should be paid off each month," Julia answered "false" (meaning, she explained, that there are times you want or need something without ready cash) and she anticipated a "false" for Jerry too. After all, he often paid the card balance over a period of months.

After both Julia and Jerry completed the questions, we compared the answers. How much of each person's attitude was shared by the other? How well did each know the other's opinions?

Not always very well, in Julia and Jerry's case. Jerry wanted to pay off credit card balances each month. He couldn't always swing it, but paying off before interest accrued was his goal. It was important to him. That and similar questions revealed not only that Jerry and Julia had never shown each other their divergent views of money but also in what ways they diverged. It is one thing to know you disagree with your spouse; it is much more helpful to know exactly where and how much you disagree.

Susan Hemfelt remembers a particular incident early in their marriage. "Robert and I considered buying a hot tub. He wanted one so badly. I thought it was impractical when we needed other things for the house. The more he pleaded his case, the more I thought a hot tub was a 'luxury' and not a 'necessity.' We 'needed' furniture that blended together as well as matching curtains.

"After we mulled the issue over and over, a new thought occurred to me: We did have enough furniture and curtains to get by, so maybe in Robert's eyes, these purchases were 'luxuries' also. Then I remembered where we first met and his need for some form of relaxation. I decided to change my position on the matter.

"Also, I decided (*and this is the key*) this was not a crucial issue that I had to win. We got the hot tub. Later the new furniture and curtains for the house came along.

"Wouldn't you know it, we had different preferences (and still do) for the temperature of the water. Many times I threatened to invite the neighborhood over for a shrimp boil in our hot tub that Robert keeps so hot! But, it's his toy. I relinquished control on this one."

How About You?

How about you and your spouse? What issues really matter to you? What issues are critical for your mate? Discuss them. Make sure these issues are ones that affect the foundation and growth of your relationship long-term. More importantly, be ready to compromise or let go of those that won't matter (much less be remembered) later.

And what are your views of family finances? What are your spouse's? This excerpt from *Getting Ready for Marriage* might reveal some ghosts from your or your spouse's past. Check the statements that apply to you:

_____ "My parents were extremely cautious about going into debt."

_____ "In my family we seldom used the air conditioner at home so we could save money."

_____ "My parents frequently fought over how to spend their money."

_____ "Having the latest styles of clothing was very important in my family."

_____ "My father usually left a good tip for the waitress/waiter in a restaurant."

_____ "My mother would give us money and say, 'Now don't tell your father.' "[1]

A second series of questions, then, reflects each of the couple's present attitudes:

_____ "It is important to me that we have a budget and try to live within it."

_____ "I think we should shop for lower prices whenever possible."

_____ "It would upset me to find out my marriage partner had money or debts I didn't know about."

_____ "I am unconcerned about money and tend not to worry about financial matters."

_____ "I want us and our children to have the latest fashions if we can afford them."

_____ "I think it is okay to ask our parents for financial help."[2]

Can you see any similarity between your answers to the first six statements and your answers to the second set? Are

some of these financial matters causing any tension between you and your spouse?

With this knowledge, the couple can now sit down and
answer a third group of questions together, such as "Who
will manage our money?" Neither Jerry nor Julia had really
thought about that, each assuming the other would not see
it as a divisive issue. "How many credit cards are *too*
many?" was another question. Julia didn't think you could
have too many.

"What about spending for recreational activities?" Julia
rated the need and pleasure of the moment most highly;
Jerry hoarded for the future. "This is the future!" Julia
protested. "Tell me that when you're sixty-five," Jerry re-
torted. The purpose of this bank of questions is to bring
the couple together into a shared attitude toward finances.

Julia and Jerry's attitudes were actually not all that wildly
divergent; the differences were subtle, wedging between
them quietly, causing discord on some occasions but not
others. Probing questions and careful attention to the answers revealed the differences so that they could be examined in the clear light of day. Only when Julia and Jerry
both knew where the differences lurked could they hope to
talk them through and resolve them.

Attitude Check

If you are in this passage you might want to review your
own attitude toward finances as a couple. Consider these
questions together:

1. Will we both work after children are born?
   _____ yes   _____ no
2. Should we have separate bank accounts?
   _____ yes   _____ no
3. Should we have separate savings accounts?
   _____ yes   _____ no

4. Should we have insurance—life, medical, car, household?

_____ yes   _____ no

How much insurance do we need? _____

5. How many credit cards are too many? _____ [3]

Finally, we often suggest that a couple enter into a financial covenant with one another, just as Jerry and Julia did, no matter where they are in the passages of marriage. Are you and your spouse willing to establish a covenant which will help eliminate any ghosts from your past? Consider a verbal or written agreement like the one below:

_____ "I agree that money will never be more important than our relationship."

_____ "I agree to let you know if I think that either of us is becoming irresponsible about financial matters."

_____ "I agree to stay within the budget we plan together."

_____ "I agree that from our wedding on, money is ours and the problems and joys it brings are also ours to share."

_____ "I agree that credit cards can be a major problem, and I'll always talk to you before making a purchase over $ _____ ."

_____ "I agree to work with you until we agree on how to pay, and who will pay, the bills in our marriage."[4]

This type of agreement between you and your spouse will help you to eliminate financial ghosts from your past. We often suggest that a couple explore their family ties in many other areas, such as communication, attitudes, and religion. If your exploration of family finances has revealed some ghosts from your past, you might want to work through *Getting Ready for Marriage*. This type of introspection is the first step toward completing the first task of this passage. Two other steps are necessary to mold you into one family unit: saying good-bye to any pain from your childhood and shifting your priorities to your new family.

Saying Good-bye

Part of pulling up those old family roots is saying good-bye to the pain of your childhood.

Other books, such as *Love Is a Choice*, deal at length with a curious phenomenon Minirth-Meier counselors see constantly. That is, the more dysfunctional and unsatisfying a child's family of origin has been, the harder it is for the child to leave it. Logic suggests that if the original family failed to serve that person's needs, leaving home is the solution. But human beings do not operate on logic. More than 80 percent of our decisions are made below the conscious level, in the deep recesses of thought and subthought where logic never goes. At the emotional level, the pain of unresolved dysfunction in the family of origin may repeatedly pull us back into enmeshment with that family or propel us to recreate that pain in our new adult relationships.

Julia Karris's mother worked ten-hour days advancing herself as a mid-level manager in a bank before coming home to the housework. Julia's father put in his eight-hour shift, then spent another three or four hours taking hands-on computer courses at the local technical school. After all, his wife was still at work anyway, so why rush home?

For all practical purposes, abandoned, Julia couldn't wait to get out of the house and on her own. Yet, once married, she called Mom and Dad three and four times a week. She dragged Rick and the kids over to the house every Sunday afternoon. In short, she kept her roots deeply ensnared in her family of origin, seeking nourishment that never had been and was never going to be.

Julia had been out of her parents' house long before she met Rick. She had made her own living, having cut economic ties with her parents. Yet emotionally, she was still her parents' little girl, still under the family-of-origin roof.

We frequently find adult children who, like Julia, have remained overinvolved with their parents. Frequently, too, the parents become so enmeshed in their children that they are loathe to give them up. Such was the case of a newly-wed named Marla. Her father died when she was nine. As she matured, an only child, she and her mother descended into a frenetic love-hate relationship.

Marla married to get away, but not very far away. She and her husband lived across town. Marla's mother felt free to pop in on them any time, for any reason or for no reason at all. "Oh, don't bother," she would say as she barged in. "It's only me." Unfortunately, Marla had become so codependently involved with Mom that she didn't realize how badly Mom was overstepping and destroying their personal boundaries.

Wearied beyond patience by this invasion of his privacy, her husband found a job in Minneapolis and summarily carted Marla off a thousand miles from her mommy. Six months later the widow retired. To Minnesota.

Few young adults are so unhealthily enmeshed with parents, but even in the most benign of relationships, friction sparks. Usually the problems, however mild, start in courtship. Conflicts erupt in wedding preparations. Annie remembers, "Beth Anne really surprised me. When she and Alan announced their marriage plans, they wanted a simple ceremony—just family and a few close friends. My only daughter without a full-blown wedding! A marriage should be celebrated in style. We could afford it, so why not?"

Beth Anne detested plans and arrangements of any sort. Annie, on the other hand, practically thrived on them. Always on committees at the church, civic organizations, or at the school, she loved to orchestrate a function and see it go off successfully. Her only daughter's wedding was the epitome of her career.

Fortunately Beth Anne and Alan weren't that attached to a certain wedding, just to each other. So when Annie explained she would be happy to handle all the arrangements —"Just leave everything to me"—Beth Anne was willing to compromise on her style of wedding.

What is actually happening in these conflicts is that daughter is pulling away from mother, son is breaking out from under his parents' roof and aegis. It is a healthy and temporary friction, unavoidable, necessary. Shifting from the old, familiar family to a new and untried family causes a wrenching jolt. As earthquakes dissipate the energy of shifting continents, so tensions and flare-ups ease the shift to the sometimes frightening new life-style.

Normally, the difficulty will be fleeting, perhaps only in adolescence or young adulthood. Annie smiled grimly. "Beth Anne was a real pill her senior year of high school. Threatened to leave home early, chafed against every rule we had. She was out on her own less than a year when the phone calls and letters got more frequent. She started coming home from college some weekends—and bringing her laundry, of course. I thought for a while, around her high school graduation, that we had lost her. But she came back, and our relationship is warmer than ever."

One of the biggest accomplishments during this time is simply leaving home. When Beth Anne entered college, she took with her the essentials she required for life away from home. Her grandfather Carl studied her overloaded minivan and suggested with a laconic smirk that she wasn't leaving home at all; she was taking it with her.

This was a far bigger move for Beth Anne than she would realize. Leaving home residentially is more than a step forward in individualization. It is also an important step toward learning to love. When we initially assess patients in the clinic, one of the things we look for at first is whether the adult client has left home residentially, financially, and in other ways.

Some of those other ways a client should have left home are socially, vocationally and avocationally, and in the realm of civic identity—that is, who am I in the community?

Beth Anne, for example, joined a sorority. Neither of her parents were Greeks. She starred in high school and college volleyball. Her mom claimed to be a klutz at anything athletic, and her father was more into intellectual pursuits—a member of the chess team, not the sports teams. Beth Anne majored in business because she wanted to do the same sort of thing her mom did—not because she wanted to follow in Mom's footsteps, but because she had seen her mom's job from the inside, so to speak, and she liked it.

Thus, Beth Anne followed her parents in some regards and departed their paths in others. The important thing was, she was beginning to listen to her own drummer.

What this all comes to, you see, is a solid sense of self. The more secure the sense of self, the more ready that person is for love. Persons who fail to emerge as independent entities in this important first passage of marriage will try to find and complete their identities through the identities of their mates. And that, the heart of codependency problems, makes for an unhealthy and unstable marital relationship.

Once the couple has successfully uprooted from their original families, attention shifts to the new family.

The New Family

Marla in Minnesota had to become a tightrope walker. You've seen the high-wire balancing acts at the circus. Some of them feature a comic performer, a person who, although highly skilled, pretends to be a novice. As he steps out onto the wire he wobbles crazily; the crowd giggles. He "falls," bouncing on the wire; the crowd gasps. He extends his arms and waves them up and down, lurching back and forth. The crowd waits for the inevitable fall.

The audience understands this parody of proper balance because a novice would do exactly those things—wobble precariously, flail wildly, fail to find the center of balance, move in fits and jerks rather than smoothly. Novices in marriage also do those things as they seek a comfortable balance between all their new and altered relationships.

In shifting to their new family, and in putting original family patterns behind, the couple in the first flush of new love must completely reshape all their other relationships. Finding the new balance point is inevitably rocky. You've never seen such wild flailing and tilting! They have to bring new balance to . . .

Relationships with the Family of Origin

A traditional Navajo husband will never look at his mother-in-law or speak to her. Even when driving her to town, he'll stay in the cab of his pick-up while she sits in the back, riding the fifty or so many miles in the open air.

Think also of all those stale Henny Youngman mother-in-law jokes. In-law conflicts and adjustments, though, are far more delicate, and can be far more rewarding, than the jokes and customs suggest.

Here you are in a whole new family, all of whose members know your spouse better than you do. They fit together like an old shoe; you feel like a cellist in a drum-and-bugle corps. There is no formula for adjusting to the in-laws. Each case is individual, each situation unique in its way. That makes finding balance all the harder. The balance becomes nearly impossible until both newlyweds successfully pull up roots from the old home.

To all these tugs between the couple and the in-laws, you can add the new relationship with siblings. Brothers and sisters are no longer the main same-generation support people. And yet, their roles, though changed drastically, should not diminish. More balancing.

Then there are the many other relationships that you had before you were married; they, too, will change.

Relationships with Single Friends

She still wants to run around with her single girlfriends, shopping, perhaps, or just doing what they used to do together, and for the best of reasons: These are her friends. He yearns for his boys' night out with the old, familiar buddies, where guys can be themselves in all their take-me-as-I-am glory.

And how about a foursome or party? It used to be that the guests had to be compatible with only the host or hostess. Now the guests have to be compatible with the couple. In a foursome, he and she both have to mesh satisfactorily with their guests. It isn't easy. Finding other couples who fit well as couples becomes quite a complex process, with lots of false starts and disappointments.

Speaking of singles, both partners must say good-bye to past romantic relationships and dreams. The infamous bachelor party symbolizes the joking but not-so-joking "This is your last fling, pal" end of an era. Raucous as such parties are, they are sad too. The groom-to-be rightfully grieves his loss of the past even as he rejoices in the many advantages his future promises.

The balance is never perfect. Personalities clash. The newlyweds find themselves embroiled in far more than just love spats. The second task of the First Passage of marriage is to deal with the inevitable conflict that's part of any relationship.

Chapter 4

Who's in Control?

C arl Warden sat on neighbor Bert's front porch as Bert boasted, "Meg and I had a perfect marriage. We never fought."

"Wish I could say that," Carl sniffed. "Bess and I, we've had some go-arounds, let me tell you! We kept it honest, though, and it all worked out."

"Not us, no sir." Bert's rocking chair squeaked with every oscillation. "Meg was the proper wife of Scripture—submissive."

Carl thought about that a few minutes and shook his head. "Bess has a mind of her own, and when she thinks I'm wrong, she doesn't hesitate a bit to point it out. I would've made some major mistakes if Bess weren't as strong as she is." Carl didn't say any more, but he reflected, *It's God's blessing to me that she doesn't let herself be a doormat.* And the recollections of Bess's solid, stubborn love nearly brought tears to his eyes.

The Second Task: To Overcome the Tendency to

Jockey for Control

The second task is one which will resurface off and on throughout all the passages of marriage. Each spouse will ask, "Who's in control here?" as different situations arise, from the choice of a restaurant for a Friday night date to the purchase of a new home. The source of conflict will change, as will the couple's methods of responding to it, but conflict itself is present in all relationships.

Unfortunately, too many couples think, *We must squelch conflict, lest it damage this relationship.* The couple instinctively know the relationship is untested and unhardened. Yet here's an equation we've learned is valid:

$$1 \text{ person} + 1 \text{ person} = \text{conflict}$$

Its corollary:

1 person-in-love + 1 person-in-love = conflict anyway

Conflict is inevitable, no matter what the ages or backgrounds. The new couple are not far enough into their relationship to know that conflict, because it is inevitable, is nothing more than a normal part of marriage. How the couple deal with that conflict, however, can make or break the union. Often their ability to handle conflict is stifled by their fragile egos and dreams.

Fragile Egos

If the couple as well as the relationship are young in years, they don't know themselves well yet. An older couple such as Louie and Marj Ajanian won't have such fragile egos. The sum of their years is more than a century; they know by now what they can do and who they are.

Even the well-established ego gets bruised at the beginning of a marital relationship.

Both parties are equally affected, of course. The man, too, enters marriage with a lot of insecurities. "Will she get

tired of me? Continue to love me? Can I satisfy her—and
keep on satisfying her? Can I handle this new responsibility? Especially, can I provide financially for her?"

One of our clients voiced those insecurities: "I felt vulnerable. If I flubbed up, if I didn't do everything expected
of a man, my ego would really take a beating. I wanted to
be the dream husband, the Clark Gable of married men."

Fragile Dreams

Not even Clark Gable the actual man could equal Clark
Gable the dream image. No matter how well the partners
think they know each other, when courtship becomes marriage, some disillusionment sets in.

Debi Newman explains it from experience. "Brian was so
romantic! In July, six months before our wedding, he sent
me six red roses. August, five months before the wedding,
five roses. And so on until one rose a month before. Janu-
ary when we got married, nothing. And for the next three
years I got nothing.

"Brian was still very nice and thoughtful toward all the
other people in his life. I felt sort of left out. We've each
given on this issue; he's more attentive, and I've learned to
be content in his love, without a rose a month."

Not just expectations transfer from courtship into marriage. So does every unresolved issue. Conflicts the couple
thought would disappear, little things in their courtship,
blossom into big things in the marriage.

Attitude Adjustment in Conflict

The couple in the throes of new love, not yet fully comfortable with each other, will instinctively guard what they
say and do. They know (although they might not articulate
that knowledge) that the greater the openness, the greater
the potential for conflict. What they may not realize is, the

greater the openness, the greater the potential for improved intimacy.

In forty-three years of marriage, Bert and Meg never achieved anything near deep intimacy. Although Bert would tell you quite truthfully that he loved his Meg, he could not tell you what Meg thought, how she responded to a situation ("Oh, I don't know, I guess she just sort of accepted it"), what she felt or when ("Frankly, she got to be something of a cold fish after a while"), or whether she even had any hopes and dreams ("Never mentioned them, so I guess she didn't have any"). And yet, every human being not only possesses a wonderful capacity for deep intimacy, every person craves it. Intimacy feeds happiness and contentment. We were made for it.

When Carl said he and Bess "kept it honest" he referred to their mutual desire to avoid dirty fighting. Conflict approached wrongly causes not intimacy but pain and alienation, separation. It's a lady-and-the-tiger situation. In a famous short story, a man must choose between two doors. If he opens the one, a willing and lovely lady awaits him. Behind the other door waits a hungry tiger. The story is an allegory of life and also typifies conflict: behind one door, intimacy; behind the other, separation. But there's an infinite difference here. The man could not know in advance which door hid what. You can.

Causes and Symptoms

Boy, do you feel rotten! Sneezing, a runny nose sore from so much blowing, no energy, aching all over. You take cold medicine, but unlike many medicines, cold medicine does nothing to cure the cold. All the king's horses and all the king's men have not been able to cure the common cold. The medicine alleviates the symptoms somewhat —the nose does not run so fast and so far, the sneezing lessens, the aches abate. But the causative agent, the cold virus, follows its merry course unhindered.

The germs cause the symptoms. Instead of that nasty cold, should you contract one of certain treatable kinds of pneumonia, the appropriate antibiotics will stop the cause —the pneumococcus germs—and thereby the symptoms as well.

Married couples assume that conflict in their union causes separation. Actually, conflict is usually not a cause; it's a symptom. The wedge has already been driven in somewhere, somehow, and conflict has resulted. We've learned that if you can find and deal with the issue causing separation—the germs, by analogy—the conflict, the symptom, takes care of itself.

Not always, though, can you do that. Sometimes you can merely treat the symptoms. However, if you handle the conflict well, improved intimacy and contentment result, and the cause emerges, to be healed.

"Aha!" you say. "So if I let 'er rip and encourage conflict, my marriage will grow stronger. Good! I love to argue."

That's not what we're saying at all! We're saying that you can turn the friction inevitable in any honest union into an asset. Food is a good illustration. We must have it; eat or die. And yet, used wrongly, food becomes the center of all sorts of problems, from anorexia to obesity.

As the marriage matures, moving from passage to passage, the couple's attitudes toward conflict will change. The symptoms—the conflicts themselves—will change somewhat. So, therefore, will the means of dealing with them.

Frank Minirth puts it this way: "Part of the idealism in the first stage is, 'We're not supposed to be fighting.' I was small as a child, and very lonely growing up. I met Mary Alice, and she was the most beautiful thing. She looked just like Snow White. How can you fight with Snow White?

"Also, fighting is a fearful thing. You just know it will destroy that fragile relationship. At first we didn't know how to handle it. We learned together how to argue without hurting each other, to grieve the past, and take up the new."

The Resolution

Although the couple's attitude toward conflict matures and changes, the three ways to handle disagreement remain the same: a) compromise, b) agreement to disagree, and c) love gift.

Compromise

Everyone gives in a little. That's what Frank and Mary Alice Minirth decided to do when they purchased a vacation home. A friend of the Minirths' tells about their compromise: "Frank is a country boy. He likes animals, he likes rural living. Mary Alice is strictly a city girl. They have a property in rural Arkansas—I mean, *very* rural Arkansas. Cabins, horses, wild land. As you approach, you see no power poles, no hints of modern conveniences at all. It looks like a hundred and fifty years ago. But inside the cabins are up-to-the-minute kitchen appliances, right down to the dishwasher and microwave. The outside is Frank's concept of country living; the inside is Mary Alice's. It's a lovely compromise and works beautifully for both of them."

Agreement to Disagree

Early in their marriage the Newmans agreed to disagree. Brian remembers one incident clearly: "Debi was making pancakes for breakfast, shortly after we married. She tossed the flour into the blender, and then an egg and some milk. That just floored me! That's not the way you do it. You mix the dry ingredients thoroughly and separately. You blend the egg into the milk. Then you slowly add the dry ingredients to the egg-and-milk until you get a perfect batter."

Debi adds: "I could have backed off and done it his way, but the potential was there for me to bury my anger—to be resentful. That wouldn't have done either one of us any good. I stuck with my way. We didn't resolve it by compromise or giving in. We simply agreed to disagree."

Brian continues: "Her pancakes turned out just fine. You know, though, a strongly controlling man might not be able to eat them when they weren't made the way he thought was 'right.'"

The symptom in that case was a disagreement over method. The cause was, again, a family-of-origin habit. Brian grew up with a certain concept of what's "right." Debi didn't mind a bit taking shortcuts.

Debi explains: "When one spouse is very controlling, it's important that the other not constantly cave in just to avoid conflict. That's an open door to unhealthy polarization. The controlling spouse becomes all the more controlling, and the other begins to lose identity and self-esteem. The situation—giving in, I mean—certainly generates anger, and that's not good for either the spouses or the marriage."

Does that mean one should never give in? Not at all!

Love Gift

A love gift is, essentially, exactly that: giving in. A love gift says, "For whatever reason, I'm giving on this issue. I may feel as strongly as you do, but I'm willing to give."

Obviously, a love gift must be given without anger or it will not be a healthy response.

Debi Newman recalls this illustration: "A situation came up when we were engaged that nearly wrecked us before we even married. I wanted to apply for a job as secretary. Brian worked as a janitor in the same building. He saw how the men treated the position of secretary—their attitude—

and the way they flirted with the secretaries. He felt extremely threatened and insecure, and he thought a couple just starting out shouldn't be in a threatening position of that sort. I wanted the security of a steady job and didn't feel I had many options.

"For a while we thought it really was the end of the relationship. Compromise wasn't possible; either I took the job or I didn't. I finally made the decision to give in on this issue. I didn't understand everything Brian was feeling; I definitely didn't agree with him, but I chose not to apply for the job out of love for him.

"God worked in all of this. He helped us with the anger and forgiveness, and I got an even better job. Surviving that crisis put us on a much deeper level of intimacy."

None of these three is appropriate to every situation. Sometimes, for example, compromise is wisest; at other times it's not possible. Should a couple become locked into one of these three approaches to the exclusion of the other two, problems follow.

Carl's friends Bert and Meg illustrate this. Meg gave in every time. And that's where a love gift became, with time, a cop-out, no longer either love or a gift.

The Nuts and Bolts of Conflict Resolution

There is no cookbook method to deal with conflict, and for good reason: In the heat of disagreement, when your very self is on the line, you don't think of following rules. And if you do think of it, you don't want to anyway, lest by following the rules you lose.

There are, however, some guidelines to prevent conflict from causing separation.

As you consider those guidelines, use as a specific example the last conflict you suffered with your spouse. It needn't be a big one—maybe it was an argument over how you spend your time. Sometimes one spouse or the other acts as if he or she is still single. The person hasn't made changes in his or her relationships with single friends as we suggested in the last chapter. "You're not playing golf again with the guys this Saturday," the wife moans. "You played golf twice this week after work. We never spend any time together." And there begins an argument.

As we go along, apply the guidelines to the particular instance you select. You'll study who said precisely what (it's amazing how often statements are misheard and misread), what the underlying feelings and needs are, what went wrong, and how you might handle the situation better when it pops up again. Because most conflicts are born of the same problems, they do keep popping up, again and again.

Know Thyself

First, understand and be aware of what's going on inside yourself. Divide a piece of paper in half vertically. On one side list the things you say out loud, such as:

- "I see you less now than I did when we were dating."
- "Who's more important to you, the guys or me?"
- "I don't matter to you; you don't really love me."

On the other side of the paper list the thoughts you are thinking:

- *He wishes he wasn't married.*
- *He'd rather be playing golf with the boys than spending time with me.*
- *I feel lonely (abandoned).*
- *I have no control over this situation.*

Often you won't admit these thoughts, but you know they are there, and now's the time to own up to these feelings.

Now think about why you might have felt that way. For example, at a pause in a wild argument, when vitriol had reached an emotional level, one of our clients suddenly sensed his old inadequacy fears kicking up. He was deeply, viscerally afraid of seeing himself as a loser. The self-revelation forced him to yield somewhat, simply to beat down that ogre from his past—inadequacy.

"I felt (lonely) _____ during this argument."
Can you remember the last time you felt that way *(for instance, "I always felt lonely when my parents went on long business trips and left me at home." Or "My father was a workaholic and he never spent much time with me.")?* I felt this way when _____."
Are these two situations similar? _____ yes _____ no
If so, how? *(For instance, the feeling is the same; "I feel as if I've been abandoned. Those feelings from childhood might be making me feel worse now.")* _____

You obtain insight into conflict in marriage through this type of introspection, through feedback from others, through willingness to grab hold of nuggets of truth others give you. You may have to wade through a lot of dross to find those nuggets. You don't have to buy it all, but do look for them. As you open yourself up to understanding, you set a precedent for how you'll resolve conflict.

Brian Newman did that. "I told a friend about the pancake incident not long after it happened. 'Brian,' he said, 'that is an amoral issue. There is no right or wrong. Don't let amoral issues become bones of contention.' He said a lot of other things, too, but that stuck with me."

The issue in Brian's case was disagreement over a method of making pancakes. His friend's input advised him on the significance of this issue. Distinguishing between a true mountain and merely a molehill is hard when you're climbing on the side of one. But becoming flexible on minor issues is critical.

Charles Swindoll, the beloved author, goes further by

implying that flexibility leads to a happy, creative and humorous family life. He even suggests saying yes to each other's ways of doing things unless it is impossible to do so.

Who knows what wild ideas or ingenuous notions will surface? And a failure is not the end of the world. If something flops, try something else. To quote the hackneyed phrase, "When life hands you lemons, make lemonade." Part of the many benefits of becoming a couple is that there are now two creative minds working together on common issues instead of one. Being open to your mate's creativity opens your own mind up to other possibilities.

Think

Have you ever analyzed a television series episode? Try it sometime. You'll find an unvarying pattern. For example, there's the one-hour adventure story: In the first two minutes, a lot of attention-getting things happen. They want you to stay at that spot on your channel selector. The plot gets rolling in a hurry, drawing you into the story. The first commercial break happens at, literally, an odd moment. The second, though, will occur on the half-hour. Just before this break, the hero will be in the utmost danger, the ultimate pits—whatever—for the producers want you involved enough that you won't switch channels during all those commercials. If there is any character development, it will happen during the third segment, "garbage time." After the third commercial break, just as it appears the villain might win, the action will lead to a flip-flop as the hero comes out on top, an exciting finish, and the wrap-up. Every time.

This is one of several reasons Americans no longer feel any strong need to think. Television, by rote formula, does all the work of thinking for us. Some shows even do the philosophizing for us in the wrap-up. We need not bother to look for deeper meanings; they are clearly explained. Yet unless people are trained in the ability to look at options and to think, they can't resolve conflicts.

"Okay," you say, "so what's to think about?"

For starters, think about what your spouse's position really is. Use debating skills. Anyone surviving a high school debating course knows that you must be able to debate either side of a question if you're to present your own side effectively. You must know where the other side's strengths and weaknesses lie. Take a moment and mentally fill in these blanks:

> "My spouse kept saying (*"You don't appreciate all I do for you or how hard I work"*): _____."
>
> "His (her) position has some merit, in that (*"he does work hard and some of the times he was playing golf he was with clients"*) _____."
>
> "He (she) seemed to be feeling (*angry, afraid*) _____."

Often the husband realizes that the wife is right. He has been spending a lot of time playing golf. So he becomes defensive because he feels guilty. He is, in fact, having difficulty making the adjustment to a married relationship where he has to consider someone else's desires.

Finally, think about those time-release capsules. Could some other situation be feeding your husband's or wife's anger?

> "I suspect that some of these feelings might have been prompted by something else besides our argument (*such as a difficult situation at work or a domineering mother who tried to control every minute of his or her time*) _____
> _____."

Frequently we are so busy formulating our own position and mentally framing the perfect riposte, we miss the other person's position completely. This type of introspection forces us to think also of just how our own side looks. (For instance, Charles Darwin, when making major decisions, would list all the pros and cons side by side. He used the method only to clarify his thoughts, and not as a guide, for although the cons far outweighed the pros, he boarded the *Beagle* anyway, and became one of the best-known figures in history.)

While you're enumerating various sides, study your own.

In your recent fight, for instance, what did you say more than once? *("You don't really love me, and I'm not sure I even love you.")* _____

Do you really know that your husband or wife doesn't love you? Do you have the power to read his or her mind? We always advise couples to stick to the facts, not their assumptions, which might well be inaccurate.

Think about the second part of that statement now: "I'm not sure I even love you."

How might that have been misconstrued? *("He or she might see those words as rejection and a threat to our marriage.")* _____
_____

Do you say these same things at other times when you and your spouse fight? _____ yes _____ no

It's natural to throw grenades back and forth in an argument. If both parties know themselves, however, they can call a halt to general accusations and talk about their true interior feelings. This will *never* happen if you speak in absolutes: "You *never* stay home with me." "You would *always* prefer playing golf with the boys rather than spending time with me."

Absolute statements usually guarantee defensiveness because they are so overstated. A husband might play golf with the boys on Saturday and once or twice during the week, but the other four nights he is at home with his spouse.

We also advise couples to be wary of character assassinations. The wife in this example might say, "You're a totally selfish person. You never think of anyone but yourself."

We suggest that couples ask themselves an important question as they are fighting: *How would you feel if your spouse said these things to you*? If you can take a moment to do this, you will readily see that you were caught in the trap of making absolute statements or dealing in character assassination.

Evaluate your own need to control. At the heart of the golfing argument is that question, "Who's in control here? Who sets the schedule? What time is mine? What time is yours? And what time is ours together?"

And much of each spouse's reaction is motivated by fear. It's scary to yield some control of your life to someone else. It's difficult to work out time-sharing in a marriage.

If you have by nature a strongly controlling personality, your potential for conflict is greater, for you feel the urge to control what you cannot control—your spouse's attitudes, feelings, and actions. We find this equally true for men and women.

And what about your husband's need for control? In the golfing example, the husband is probably feeling, *You're trying to control every part of my life*. He's just as afraid as you are.

Finally keep a clear head about just how big this fight really is. Not all disagreements are created equal.

Susan Hemfelt recounts this from her past.

"My parents disagreed in a civil manner in front of us kids, but it was never a strong fight. They drew the line between disagreement and a screaming mimi. Their philosophy was don't fight in front of kids.

"Oh, we knew they disagreed sometimes. But we also

knew growing up that they respected each other. They were united but not rigid about it. I mean, some things were privately negotiable. But they never dragged us kids into it."

If you were looking at that fight from the perspective of six months from now, would it rate as an enormous barrier or an insignificant pothole on the road to happiness?

Stick to the Basics

Think also about the basics. Vince Lombardi watched his Green Bay Packers lose several games and decided to go back to basics. He waved a pigskin aloft and announced, "This is a football."

Julia Karris wanted to buy her stepdaughter, Kinsley, the latest shoes for school. Jerry insisted that sixty-nine dollars was too much for a pair of shoes the fourteen-year-old was going to outgrow by Christmas.

Julia explained the prestige attached to that particular brand.

Jerry remained unimpressed. He lauded frugality.

So far, both were sticking to the basics.

Then Julia pointed out how much Jerry spent for fishing equipment. He countered with the amount of "free" time she gave the department store. She complained how stingy he was, and he fumed that she shared the same spendthrift ways that alienated him from his first wife. Basics had just gone out the window.

Caught in the middle, young Kinsley felt certain she was the cause of her parents' fight. She could not see, nor could they, that they had strayed from the basics. They were dragging in issues from the past, things which have nothing whatever to do with the wisdom of purchasing a pair of shoes.

When Carl and Bess "kept it honest" as they fought, Carl meant essentially that they thought about the basics. *They kept to the issue at hand*. If the price of a pair of shoes were at issue, they argued the cost and value of the shoes. And that brings up another key point Julia and Jerry were missing.

Keep Your Self Out of It

"Keep out of it? But we're the ones fighting!"

Issues and persons are two different things. *Argue over issues, but never allow your conflict to get personal.* As much as you can, keep emotions out of it. Given its own way, the need to win will gain full control of your emotions and rob your rational processes. Disagreement then becomes a brute dogfight, invariably shredding love and egos. Dogs don't fight in support of ideas; they fight each other. A constant equation here:

$$\text{Conflict} - \text{rational processes} = \text{explosion}$$

Brian Newman says: "We see it constantly in couples we counsel. Once a conflict becomes emotional, reason goes out the door and the conflict is never going to be resolved. We help the couple keep it from becoming personal, by any of several ways."

Get Creative

Part of being creative about conflict is being able to see options. There is, for example, the obvious but rarely used option to simply cool off a while.

Debi explains: "So very frequently when we talk to Christian couples, we hear the passage, 'Be angry, but do not sin; do not let the sun go down on your anger.' The man and woman interpret it that their anger has to be resolved quickly, and so they deny their anger. Or else, they take it to bed with them. Lights out may be the first time the couple is really together.

"We try to help them see that dealing with anger does not always mean getting rid of it or resolving it right away. That's simply not possible in every instance. By all means, address the anger before the sun goes down. But you might have to address it by agreeing to not deal with it now; you'll deal with it tomorrow. Then set a definite time tomorrow. You may not be able to sleep any better, but it gives you breathing space."

Frank Minirth agrees: "Don't lie in bed, tired and frustrated, and expect to hash it out, whatever it is. You don't have the ability to look at options then. To be creative in dealing with conflict, you must be fresh enough to think."

Breathing space. Time-out. Most people need to dispel the physical rush with which anger and frustration can overload the rational circuits. Skip rocks on the pond, mow the lawn, do something physical to sap off the adrenaline that anger ignited. Indeed, you may have to postpone discussion more than once if the flame isn't banked right away.

Cooling-off time is not wasted time. There are many helpful things a couple might want to do during such a time-out, such as write your spouse an uncensored, ventilation letter. Don't mail this. It serves its purpose just by being written. Flush it down the toilet with military honors.

Defuse the Situation

One couple hit upon a diversion by accident. In a particularly acrimonious set-to, the bride of seven months wailed, "All I know how to do is love!" Now one or the other will pop that quote into the middle of an argument, and they both end up giggling. Situation defused.

Another couple take their clothes off if argument rains hard and heavy. It is very difficult to argue angrily in the nude. The sheer incongruity of the situation works against anger.

Reflect now on that fight we've been picking apart in this section. Should something have been done to prevent its escalation? What could have you done?

"I could have (*called time out by going outside to do some yard work or I could have given up trying to control the situation*)." _____

_____

Sometimes fights are the only way two people express their true feelings. In the golfing argument, that is exactly what happened. Both spouses had a problem that needed to be aired and resolved. Did that happen in your incident? The next time the issue surfaces, what are three different ways you can redirect it, making it not a fight but a negotiating point?

For instance, if the couple in our example argument worked through their fears—his about her controlling him as his mother did, and hers about being neglected as she was as a child, and the natural fear of giving up some control of their lives in the intimate relationship of marriage—they can then negotiate a workable solution. The wife might say, "If you play golf once—or at the most twice—a week, then you and I also need to have a date, where you are investing some time with me." Unless their underlying fears are shared with one another, however, this healthy resolution will never occur.

Think about your incident now. What can you do next to redirect the argument to make the experience beneficial to you and your spouse?

I could:

1. _____
2. _____
3. _____

The Bottom Line

Although you cannot always expect perfect resolution, you must always look toward eventual resolution. The alternatives are easily seen in those mathematical equations:

Conflict − resolution = separation.
Conflict + resolution = intimacy.

The argument unsettled, the opinion unvoiced, the issue unresolved—all such un's become wedges between a couple. If a couple formally separates, we have found, that the final separation actually began long before through a long series of mini-separations; in fact, sometimes from the very beginning of the marriage.

The balance is never perfect. Personalities clash. The newlyweds find themselves embroiled in far more than just love spats.

A friend of Italian extraction, with a large, close-knit family, spoke proudly of his kin. "We're what they call an extended family—grandparents, cousins, and all that. We get together every Sunday. My wife calls it the weekly gang war. We argue and laugh and snarl at each other and hug each other. I don't know how to explain it. She was raised to hide differences of opinion. We've always trotted the arguments right out. She doesn't understand how we can yell at each other if we love each other."

Conflict and love, coexisting side by side. But not all conflicts are easily seen. Not all erupt as arguments.

One source of conflict that arises in this First Passage of Marriage is sexual conflict. In the next chapter we will look at the third task of this passage—to build a sexual union—which will eliminate much of this conflict.

Chapter 5

Is Your Brain Affecting Your Sexual Experience?

*S*teve Pauling was a hunk. His new wife, Sally, matched his good looks in every way. Her strawberry-blonde hair bounced and shimmered. She could slop around in a tank top and cutoffs or strut in a formal evening gown; everything she wore flattered her beautiful shape. When Steve and Sally married, their friends called it the Ken-and-Barbie wedding. Members of the wedding party sniggered as they agreed that they would have to separate the gorgeous couple with a fire hose when the honeymoon was over and Steve had to go back to work.

Six months later, Sally and Steve sat in our office. Married half a year, they were engaging in sex once a month. Or less.

"I hate it," Sally moaned. "Every night I hide in a flannel nightgown all curled up on my side and dread the thought that maybe he'll reach for me. I can't stand his touch. I can't stand. . . ." She shuddered.

"In the beginning, when our relationship first turned physical, it was great." Steve squirmed, uncomfortable. He didn't discuss sex well at all. "A couple of weeks after the wedding, it all nosedived. I mean zip. Nothing."

81

"I think I know what caused it," Sally offered. "In college I dated this guy who—well, I guess the term is date rape. The third time we went out, he forced himself on me. He kept insisting and arguing and finally just did it. He said that's what adults do when they date, and he wasn't going to be denied just because my religion made me too prim. I'm sure that's what caused this."

"Why are you so sure?" we asked her.

"I think about it so much, especially when Steve touches me. That's how I know."

Thoughts that intrude themselves the way she described can be a good indication. And we certainly know that a traumatic event such as rape—yes, date rape is rape—can profoundly influence the marriage relationship. But the answers were not nearly so cut-and-dried as Sally believed.

You see, Sally's mind, which controlled her thoughts and memories, had, quite literally, a mind of its own. We knew it could well be that the traumatic memories of that date rape covered a deeper, more severe reason for their sexual dysfunction. And as we discovered soon, it did indeed. First, Sally and Steve had to learn something about the body's most important sex organ.

The Third Task: Building a Sexual Union

In *A Passage to India,* an Englishwoman and Indian discuss arranged marriages. "But what about love?" she asks, in essence. His reply: "We were a man and a woman, and we were young."

Letting nature take its course would be sufficient, were sex primarily biological. It is not. Unlike other biological needs—food, shelter, water—the sex drive is profoundly influenced by factors outside biology. Physical factors such as drugs or alcohol, fatigue, stress, and physical disabilities alter sexual response. But the most active sex organ, and the least appreciated, is the brain. It does its thing largely beyond the conscious level. Personal problems and distractions, fear, misconceptions about sex ("hang-ups," if you will), and the emotional states of both parties are subconscious mental factors.

Today, newlyweds come to bed armed with all sorts of "safe sex" information but very little about what really happens emotionally and physiologically. Too bad, because by understanding them, you can easier sort out just what part your brain is playing in your sexual expression. And you will know how the human body responds.

The Anatomy of Sexual Intimacy

Picture a sexual episode in four phases: Desire, Excitement, Orgasm, and Resolution. A graph of the man's and woman's experience will differ in shape, for their stimuli and timing differ. "A man is turned on by what he sees, a woman by what she hears." You may have heard that before. The man can complete a satisfying sexual episode in a few brief moments; a woman requires ten minutes or more. The man and woman who understand these and other differences and adjust for them will enjoy a far firmer and more satisfying union than will the couple who disregard nuance and detail.

Desire

The first phase, desire, begins with thoughts of the spouse. Here, right at the beginning, we find differences between men and women. The sights, the sounds, the smells, an occasional kiss excite the man. Words, actions, touch, and her relationship with her husband encourage the woman's desire. His primary fear, now and later, is that his sexual performance might fall short, failing to bring his wife to orgasm, failing to complete a satisfactory episode for them both. Her fear centers upon being unwanted sexually.

If problems appear during this early phase, they are almost always the result of personal or relational problems.

Most of the time it's not a physical malfunction. We will talk about these problems in the second part of this chapter so we can cover them completely.

Excitement

During the next phase, excitement, the skin flushes. The man's scrotum and testicles shift. His penis rises to erection. So does her clitoris, as she releases a slippery, wet lubricant.

The sexual experience levels out now, which is actually a part of the excitement phase. Unless he prolongs it, a man's plateau can be extremely short. The woman's progress ambles across a relatively long plateau of some minutes. To reach orgasm, about one-third of women need their men to stroke their clitoris manually for five to fifteen minutes as their desire builds. Rather than delaying the man's ultimate pleasure, this lengthened plateau increases it. Men who wait, bringing their women to full excitement, enjoy a more intense and pleasurable orgasm.

If the problems appear during the second phase of lovemaking, the couple usually sees a physician to rule out physical causes. Alcohol and drugs, including prescription drugs for such things as blood pressure, can cripple sexual performance. Fatigue and stress splash cold water on the fires of desire. Often, so does obesity, not for physical reasons so much as for psychological ones—the man or woman feels unlovable and unsexy.

Hormonal problems, certain diseases, and medications— we make certain that doctors have ruled out any physical reasons for the body's lack of sexual response. Fifty percent of the time they will be emotional or psychological, to be resolved through counsel.

"After medical causes have been ruled out, we dig for the underlying problems," Debi Newman says. "We also use some reverse psychology. It works especially well for people having problems in this middle phase. I give them an assignment. 'This next week,' I say, 'I want you to shut yourself off in a room. Find complete privacy. Undress, massage each other, be together, touch in nonsexual areas. Tell each other what feels good. If your shoulder is tense and your partner massages it, and it feels good, tell your partner that.'

"It's an exercise to show the couple how very important communication is to sexuality. Then I tell them, 'But don't have sex. This is a nonsexual exercise.' Once you tell them they can't, they usually do. It's not just human nature. You're lowering their anxiety about it. This relieves anger and stress. Even if it doesn't result in unblocking their sexual responses, they at least have the intimate experience of touching, saying what's pleasurable. They talk their way through it, and that's a positive gain."

Orgasm

Now man and woman arrive at orgasm. He achieves ejaculation. She experiences a thrilling tingle of pleasure rippling across her. Man and woman need not reach the top simultaneously; remember, they do have different experiences.

If the sexual dysfunction surfaces in the third and ultimate phase, physiological problems may well be the cause, particularly for men who have difficulty maintaining erection. Specific dysfunctions include impotence, wherein a man folds before achieving ejaculation—that is, fails to maintain erection. He may fail to obtain an erection at all. Failure to adequately control the timing of ejaculation is called premature ejaculation. The woman may fail to achieve orgasm or reach it only very occasionally. Her outer vaginal muscles may spasm, tightening down so intensely that he cannot enter at all.

"As before," says Debi, "we look for underlying causes. However, many times we find the problem is that women, and men too, don't understand their body and its sexual functions. Each rather naturally believes, 'My spouse feels and responds as I do. What pleases me will please my spouse.' As you've seen, that's not true. In those cases, education can help a great deal. Simply explaining the function of the clitoris and how to stimulate it can sometimes solve the problem.

"The wife must tell her husband what is bringing her to a state of orgasm and how he can help her get there," advises Debi Newman. "He should also guide her into what is pleasurable for him. Open, honest exchange is absolutely essential."

A lot of fiction embellishes the fact of sexual union which can damage or delay sexual satisfaction for newlyweds (oldlyweds, too, for that matter). For example, "A good spouse never says no." Or he fears his masculinity comes into question if he doesn't perform on demand, and she fears that if he doesn't get it here whenever he wants it, he'll seek it elsewhere. In counsel we find women who feel that good girls must remain passive. But it is normal for the woman to initiate sexual activity and to participate fully.

A lot of misinformation centers around orgasm. "It's my spouse's fault if I don't have one." Maybe it is, but don't bet the ranch on it. Probably what you both need is more openness in talking about it. A man might decide a woman is incapable of it anyway, so why try. Another couple might feel that if the performance isn't athletic, it's not erotic. The man who falls victim to one or two episodes of impotence might quit trying altogether.

And then there are the romance novels and the cinema and the sheets-and-bare-shoulders TV movies. "Oh, wow, that's exciting and fulfilling and dramatic! How come we're so clumsy and awkward? Why isn't it the singing, zinging thing the novelists describe?" Keep in mind that good sex, like good golf, takes practice. Also remember that the media are not training sources; they are fantasy machines. They project a larger-than-life view of sex in order to promote the fantasy. They want to leave you breathless and wide-eyed, not better informed. The cops and robbers don't shoot real bullets in those movies, either. It's an elaborately staged set-up. Your love life is the real thing and, pursued with elan, will provide infinitely better pleasure and intimacy than any manufactured fantasy.

Resolution

In resolution, man and woman again take widely different routes. As his sexual organs return to their nonexcited condition, his body savors a rich feeling of well-being. He toboggans from mountaintop down to flat land rapidly. It's over, and his sex interest is pretty much centered on the orgasm. He will go into a refractory period now, meaning that he will not achieve orgasm again quickly. In very young men, refraction may last fifteen minutes; in older men, three days or a week or a month.

She doesn't follow that pattern at all. She is capable of multiple orgasms, and her primary sex interest centers on the closeness and emotional union the sex act provides. She will descend the mountain at a much more leisurely pace as her primary and secondary sexual organs return to their nonexcited states.

Now that we've walked through the phases of sexual intimacy, let's take a careful look at the effect that misunderstood sex organ, the brain, can have on any one of these phases, particularly the first phase, desire.

The Brain as a Sex Organ

Sally and Steve Pauling hit trouble right in that initial phase, desire. Sally turned off just thinking about him. She immediately identified one problem she would have to work through with guidance, that date rape. That's abuse. But there was more.

Sally and Steve's extremely conservative upbringing

made sex a nasty thing no one indulged in if they were nice and clean and good, the way their families expected them to be. Both members of this couple illustrate the problem factors we find most commonly.

The major factors that can influence your sexual experience are personal problems within one of the spouses and relational problems between the couple.

Problems Within a Spouse

Personal problems within one of the spouses are often related to what we call "sexual taboos," another of those old time capsules from the past.

Sexual Taboos

Possibly the most common dysfunctions a new couple must combat are the sexual taboos they learned in childhood, those deep-seated precepts, such as, "It's wrong to be sexual inside a family." They enter the couple's life when they first marry and become a family, or especially after the first child is born, for then the marriage truly is a family.

Another unconscious message is the equation:

$$Sexy = illicit$$

And the reverse is also seen as true:

$$Illicit = sexy$$

Therefore, if I'm sexy, I'm being illicit or dirty or immoral.

Soon after marriage, one or both partners shut down. One or both of them experience physical problems with intercourse or their emotional satisfaction freezes up. Sex has become domestic. And yet, because married couples are supposed to be sexual and the precept is buried too deeply to find, sex goes on, muted by the conundrum, possibly damaged, but it goes on.

We counseled a woman in her early twenties who was trapped in this passage of marriage in sexual intimacy, even though she had entered the Second Passage of Marriage chronologically. She loved her husband and was strongly attracted to him physically during courtship. But as soon as they married—in fact, within days of the ceremony—her desire went away. Oh, she dutifully continued the sex, but she received no satisfaction, felt no desire. She had no idea where the problem came from. We went back through her history to explore stated and unspoken messages. By process of elimination, the taboo "It's wrong to be sexual inside a family" emerged. Her parents had slept in separate rooms for many years, and every time she went out on a date during her dating years, her mother warned her not to get pregnant. As soon as we dealt with her sexual taboos by replacing them with the correct message that sex in a marriage is legitimate, that sex is the God-given means of union between man and wife, her inhibitions melted. The new message was something she had always known in her head. But the silent hidden message shouted down that head knowledge.

Frequently, we counsel couples whose premarital sex was far more satisfying than any they're experiencing in marriage. It's a function of that same old sex-is-dirty attitude. Since sex outside the union is perceived as wrong, and sexual abuse is not only wrong but devastating, the sex-is-dirty feeling is strongly reinforced. Suddenly, the couple say a few wedding words, throw a whiz-bang reception, and sex isn't dirty anymore. The head can make the switch, but the heart gets thrown for a loop.

During that big trend when couples were living together, another sexual taboo we call the incest inhibition wreaked havoc. Couples would apparently do well with several years of living together. Confident that they were compatible, they would formalize the union, then divorce in a few months or a year. The incest inhibition that said, "It is wrong to have sex within a family" had remained silently buried until the couple actually became an "official" family.

In the area of sexuality, as in the areas of many decisions within the new family, those time capsules from your childhood family may begin to affect your sexual intimacy.

Those Time-Release Capsules

They came in for counsel regarding sexual dysfunction. Edith could not bear to let her husband see her any way other than fully clothed. When they first married, everything was grand except for one little quirk: Any time Edith's husband saw her undress or asked her to undress or looked at her, she would become extremely uncomfortable and have to cover up. They made love in total darkness. He dismissed it at first, chalking it off to shyness in the new union. But her problem intensified, and by the second year of marriage she wore a heavy robe to bed. She could not tolerate his looking at her.

"You feel uncomfortable now. What feelings made you uncomfortable when you were young?" We started at the beginning and moved forward through Edith's life, exploring feelings and events. Her father had never sexually molested her or ever touched her wrongly or made unseemly remarks. But every now and then she'd catch Dad staring at her. His look made her squirm even now as she described it. Yet it wasn't actually leering. Repeatedly, Dad would burst into the bathroom or bedroom without knocking, catching her in states of semi-undress. There was always some legitimate reason; at least, he always had an excuse. And after all, he was her father. Even though there was no episode of molestation, Dad's interest was inappropriate, and she sensed it even in childhood. Recognizing and grieving that covert abuse helped her master her inhibition.

What about you? Analyze your parents' life-style carefully. Do so with your grandparents' also, if you're familiar at all with it. Here are a few of the statements from *Getting Ready for Marriage*. Check those that apply to your family of origin:

_____ In my family, sex was not discussed.

_____ My mother and father hugged and kissed in front of the children.

_____ My parents slept in separate beds.

_____ My parents believed that a marriage should be faithful and permanent.

_____ My family used affection as a reward for good behavior and withheld it for bad behavior.

_____ My mother thought intercourse was a wife's duty.

_____ I received excellent sexual information from my parents.

_____ I never felt free to ask my parents anything about sexual issues.[1]

Elaine is a young woman with a frigidity problem. She is certain that her husband is to blame, because she had numerous premarital lovers and enjoyed sexual expression very much then. Now, in marriage, she simply cannot warm up to the man. That hurts her too, because she's physically quite attractive, with long auburn hair and a graceful figure. And her husband would be classified as "a looker" by any female who is well experienced in making classifications of that sort. Elaine's conflict is sexual, linking back to deep-rooted family-of-origin problems.

"What does your mom think of sex?" we asked her.

"I don't know. She never talked about it."

"Never gave you the facts of life?"

"Sorta. Well, no, not really. I got most of it by trial and error. She simply insisted sex was evil and bad and I mustn't do it. No detail about what I mustn't do."

Elaine's promiscuous behavior prior to marriage seems just the opposite of her mom's reticent attitude. But in the long run, it wasn't. "Sex is valueless" was the essence of her mother's message to Elaine. And Elaine's failure to uphold appropriate values for sexual conduct was at least an emotional, if not logical, extension of her mother's original message. But Elaine's mom and dad, we learned, never made peace with each other sexually. To her mom it has always been a burden. Elaine picked up a deep unspoken message, a hidden contract: "I'm going to create a sexless marriage." This hidden contract provides a key to what prior generations failed to resolve. It also demonstrates the root of her confict.

Look back at the statements you checked on your family-of-origin's sexual attitudes. Are there any actions or attitudes in your childhood that might be influencing your married life? Think about your own attitudes toward sexuality by checking the statements below:

_____ It is important to me that we greet each other affectionately after being apart all day.

_____ I like to be held and touched without always having intercourse.

_____ I am easily embarrassed when I am nude.

_____ Sex is too embarrassing for me to talk about.

_____ I think that sex outside of marriage is okay.

_____ I believe sex should be honored within the marriage covenant.

_____ I think it's okay to use sex as a weapon or reward.

_____ I think that the woman should do whatever the man wants.

_____ I feel free to talk about my mate and our intimate sex life with my friends.

_____ It is all right for the woman to initiate sexual activity.

_____ I believe that a man should take the lead in sexual intercourse.[2]

Do you see any patterns from your childhood reflected in your present life? More important, do you see conflict in your marriage now because your spouse doesn't like your way of doing something? Or were there such conflicts in the past that are now apparently resolved? Maybe they aren't. Burying them is not the same as resolving them.

In the deepest depths of every marriage lie the real reasons for behavior. Those reasons voice themselves if you listen carefully. What is your marriage trying to tell you?

Talk about these issues with your spouse. Then consider a sexual relationship covenant, like the one below:

_____ I agree that we may differ on some things, and I agree to respect your opinion and feelings.

_____ I agree to be open and honest about our sexual relationship.

_____ I agree that the only way I can really please you is to let you guide me, and I am willing to do so.

_____ I agree not to use sex as a weapon or reward.

_____ I agree not to criticize or make fun of my mate's sexuality.

_____ I believe that God's teaching and guidelines about sexual relationships are important and agree to make them a part of our marriage.[3]

We've found that verbal or written covenants, such as this, form the foundation for an honest sexual relationship that undergirds any strong marriage.

A final personal problem, one that is extremely devastating to sexual intimacy, is previous sexual abuse.

Sexual Abuse

We have never yet seen an exception to the rule that a woman or man sexually abused in childhood will suffer some degree of sexual dysfunction in adulthood. Problems within the person include damage done by sexual abuse and other traumatic sexual experiences. Such damage almost always affects marital sex. In these cases professional counseling is almost always necessary. We also recommend reading the book *The Wounded Heart,* by Dr. Dan Allendar (Colorado Springs: NavPress, 1990).

Persons coming from a home where sex was thought of as nothing but dirty, or never mentioned at all, experience what we call passive sexual abuse. Fear or revulsion of sex and sexuality may stem from this passive abuse.

One special form of sexual abuse which may haunt a marriage is the negative emotional legacy in premarital abortion.

Abortion

The nitty-gritty of Sally and Steve Pauling's sexual problems emerged in the third session. We were talking about children when Sally blurted out, "We'd have a baby now if we didn't . . . never mind."

Alerted, we explored what that sentence had left unspoken. Sally and Steve both grew up with conservative religious beliefs that forbade sexual relations outside marriage. Despite that, they became physically intimate some months before their wedding. Sally got pregnant. Steve, unwilling and unable to deal with fatherhood at this stage in his life, encouraged Sally to have an abortion. At the time, it seemed the only way out. After all, it was perfectly legal. Had the baby come to term, it would have been born the week they entered counsel.

Here was the main issue, buried beneath the unrelated issue of date rape. Steve had refused at the time to discuss what they were doing or to talk about it after it was done. When Sally desperately wanted his support, he considered the matter finished. With counsel, she came to understand her intense resentment toward Steve, that he had not been there for her emotionally when she needed him most. She finally saw that her sexual shutdown was her only weapon, a sexual weapon, to express her resentment and punish him for his apparent coldness.

An abortion in the woman's past will sometimes cause disruption in sexual intimacy. It's supposed to be over with. Done. The wedding was going to take care of it, but the issue remains. Usually, he doesn't appreciate what the woman is going through and forgets about it, failing to recognize the intensity of her feelings. She expects him to share her grief and sense of guilt when he doesn't even recognize it as a baby. Conflict.

We know from our practices that if married persons do not resolve the special problems generated by an abortion in the past, they separate right in the beginning, emotionally if not residentially. They don't trust each other. They are hurting. The man feels threatened and the woman is carrying all the load. As we mentioned, the husband usually doesn't want to admit it was a baby. That leaves the woman to handle all the emotional, psychological, and physical trauma for both of them. Typically, he won't talk about it; threatened by her anger, he may not listen if she tries to talk about it, or he thrusts it aside. Frequently, he's reluctant to deal with the mistake at all. So he is not open to sharing what the woman is going through. It becomes a formidable barrier to intimacy and a bar to any further movement through the passages.

The first thing we do when counseling couples with an abortion in their past is to help them resolve the responsibility fifty-fifty. Then we can lead the couple into mutual grieving and mutual forgiveness. It sounds simple, easy, even glib. In reality, it is immensely difficult and painful. It takes time.

Relationship Problems

Problems in sexual intimacy also evolve from relationship problems between the husband and wife.

Infertility

Still another source of relationship problems sometimes makes itself known about now: infertility.

When baby-making time comes, in many cases nothing happens. The couple experience anxiety and doubt. Sex becomes a mechanical thing to a specific end—assume just the right position; do it at exactly the right time. The man begins to feel used. So preoccupied is she, the woman neither feels very sexy nor comes across as such.

Conflict

Problems will be generated by the marital relationship itself where anger, frustration, and resentment reside. "Conflict and lack of communication are frequent reasons for dysfunction," Debi explains. "Below the conscious level, the person yearns to get back at the spouse for real or perceived faults and slights. He or she uses sex as a tool. Often the person simply cannot perform and may not consciously know why. Withholding sex and pleasure is perhaps the only weapon that person has."

Such was the case with Steve and Sally. Unconsciously, she resented his emotional abandonment through the abortion. The only way to get back at him was to use sex as a means for punishing him for his apparent coldness. She saw finally that her sexual shutdown was her weapon against Steve.

If you harbor resentment or bitterness, your sexual activity will suffer, one way or another. This concept is so important we will explore it in detail in the next chapter and in other books on later passages of marriage.

Sex, we have found, mirrors the marriage's general health. When heavy problems and lasting dysfunctions persist, the sexual life suffers. The husband says, "If things went better in bed, everything would be all right," even as the wife says, "If we had our financial affairs in order, sex would be a lot better."

Any stressor shoving at your marriage right now can affect your sexual intimacy. Yet we don't want to suggest that every slight irregularity reflects a sexual problem. During the first two years, obviously, a great deal of sexual adjustment takes place. It is not at all uncommon for couples during that first year or two to go through phases when they shut down. They may go overboard for a few weeks and then go dormant for a few more. As a short-term dysfunction it's not really a dysfunction. They're working out a rhythm. When problems persist, though, and cannot be talked through, we urge professional counseling.

Finally, we always counsel couples to commit to love-making and romance in their marriage.

Commit to Lovemaking

Commit to lovemaking, not just as a recreational option available to married folks, but as a channel to deeper intimacy. It's one of the nicest things you and your spouse can do for each other.

But there is lovemaking and there is lovemaking.

Debi Newman points out, "There is fun sex versus meaningful sex. The world and media teach fun sex. It's exciting. In some cases the world even teaches to try different partners, which of course we certainly never would. Sex is uniquely designed for the marriage union. Outside marriage there's no commitment. That's not real intimacy. It's all physical, all on the surface. Outside the marital context, pleasure is its only goal.

"In contrast, meaningful sex is a special relationship with a particular person, an expression of emotional oneness as well as sexual release. Intimacy is the goal as well as pleasure. Sex and intimacy are not synonymous. Real intimacy is not truly available when you seek only pleasure. Intimate marital sex provides an emotional intensity greater than just the physical orgasm. Call it soul orgasm or emotional orgasm. Good marital sex gives physical pleasure secondarily."

Debi's advice is not limited to new marital partners in this First Passage. Couples should be talking about sex throughout the marriage. Sexual intimacy is a journey. Partners who focus only on pleasure are bound to be disappointed eventually because there is only so much pleasure in the physical experience. Those who focus on intimacy find that the pleasures of sex never pale.

Commit to Romance

"But you just said that," you remind us. " 'Commit to lovemaking.' "

No, we didn't, not exactly. Romance and sex are not synonymous. Romance deeply enhances sex, and sex vividly fulfills romance. Sex is lovemaking; romance is love-nurturing. Romance is holding hands, a heartfelt kiss that happened spontaneously, a rose on her pillow, a light in the window when he's coming home late. Romance is dinner for two. Most of all, romance is listening, truly listening, to the quiet of each other's heart.

As Frank Minirth puts it: "We have to move beyond Passage One in our marriage. But at the same time, we need to hold on to some of the feelings energized at this stage. We ought not lose all our idealism."

Mary Alice and Frank Minirth carve out time for each other. They date. They take walks and hold hands. Romance. The old dream dreamt anew.

How do you hang on to the romance, the idealism? Behavior helps. Do the same things you did when you dated. Walk together, hold hands. Feelings drive our behavior, but behavior also drives our feelings.

"People get in trouble when they become disillusioned.

When they see it's not perfect, they tend to bag it," Frank says.

Don't throw out idealism and romantic love, but hang on to it in the face of reality and imperfection. Work through the realism and other stages, but don't forget romantic love.

"Lose the romance? That would be a shame!"

Romance-killers

If romance is such a dandy thing, who in their right mind would ditch it? It gets scuttled by two major factors, time and conflict. As time goes by and the marriage matures, the fruits of that maturation tend to quench romance. In our other books on later passages, we will look at this phenomenon.

But conflict, now there is a romance-killer you can do something about. Many sources of conflict arrive early and stay late in the union. Some that we have talked about in Chapter 4 are:

- Whose will shall prevail, mine or my spouse's?
- How much independence and individuality is too much? Not enough?
- Who will play which roles in the marriage? Who will mow the lawn? Carve the turkey? Cook it?
- Who gets to spend the money? Make the money?
- Who will raise the kids? Whose wishes will prevail regarding parenting?
- Who gets saddled with the extended-family problems?

Ask yourself the above questions. Then consider whether any of these issues are causing strife in your relationship. Are they creating anger and resentment within you? If so, is this affecting your sexual union?

Whose will prevails most of the time, mine or my spouse's?

(For example, *I have to admit I yield 60-70 percent of the ultimate decision-making authority and I recognize that may be unfair to my spouse.*)

———————————————————————————

———————————————————————————

———————————————————————————

(This one should turn out somewhere around 50-50.)

How much independence and individuality is too much? My independence shows in the following ways. (For example, *my husband and I maintain small, separate checking accounts for personal spending. That gives me a healthy sense of financial independence.*)

———————————————————————————

———————————————————————————

———————————————————————————

My spouse shows his autonomy in the following ways. (For example, *my husband takes five or six weekends a year to go hunting and fishing with the men.*)

———————————————————————————

———————————————————————————

———————————————————————————

We overlap in the following ways. (For example, *we always plan one major shared vacation per year.*)

———————————————————————————

———————————————————————————

———————————————————————————

Now think about the overlaps. Are they comfortable? intrusive? Can they be characterized as interdependence or as enmeshment? What would make these overlaps, these examples of nonindividuality unwholesome in your eyes? (For example, do I lose my sense of self-respect when my spouse begins to assume excessive management of my day-to-day activities?)

_____

_____

_____

Who will play which roles in the marriage?
I consider these traditionally my role (*cleaning, cooking, changing the oil in the car, mowing the lawn, cleaning gutters, ordering closets, walking pets, etc.*):

1. _____
2. _____
3. _____
4. _____
5. _____
6. _____

What roles do I automatically assume my spouse should be playing?

1. _____
2. _____
3. _____
4. _____
5. _____
6. _____

Think about the items. How many are governed by your family of origin ("That's the way my parents did it") and how many by a genuine agreement in principle between yourself and your spouse? What would you like to change?

Who gets to spend the money? Make the money?

Be honest. Is this the preferred arrangement for you both? Why or why not?

_____

_____

_____

Who will raise the kids? Whose wishes and actions will prevail regarding parenting? Specifically:
Potty training: _____

When the child gets that first bike: _____

When the child sleeps over at a friend's: _____

When the child begins driving a car: _____

When the child begins dating: _____

Who gives the child haircuts? _____

Who will discipline? _____

To what degree? _____

Who gets saddled with the extended-family problems? Who's taking care of debilitated older family members? Why?

_____

_____

_____

List some personal problems family members are having:

_____

_____

_____

What are you or your spouse going to do, if anything, about them?

_____

_____

_____

They are certainly well meaning, but are these actions healthy or unwholesome, welcome or intrusive? Put bluntly, is it any of your business? Discuss the actions' possible consequences on both the family member and your own marriage.

_____

_____

_____

_____

_____

_____

Anger and resentment are so pervasive in a marriage, we will explore these two damaging and negative emotions in the next chapter.

Chapter 6

Can You Forgive and Resolve the Anger and Resentment?

"**I** forgive you for running over my goldfish in the driveway yesterday." Kinsley Karris stood in the middle of the kitchen floor.

"Thank you, Kins." Julia Karris hugged her fourteen-year-old stepdaughter. Kinsley ran off upstairs.

By the kitchen sink, Jerry gaped. "What?"

"I think it's wonderful!" Julia crossed to him. "That was the first time—the very first time—Kinsley has ever said 'I forgive you' since I've known her."

"But—?"

"Jerry, forgiveness is an essential part of living well. And it has to be learned; it's not natural. It doesn't just come."

"Okay. But, uh, a goldfish?"

"Oh. Well," said Julia with a wave of the hand, "what happened there is obvious."

Jerry stood blinking. He never did find out.

The Need to Forgive

Who are the people who say "I'll never forgive," "It's too great; I cannot forgive that"? They are the ones with ulcers, with high blood pressure, with tense relationships. Failure to forgive is poor physiology as well as poor theology—"Forgive us our trespasses as we forgive those who trespass against us." It is also very poor psychology.

To not forgive is to damage oneself.

The Results of Anger

The opposites of forgiveness are resentment and anger. Anger and resentment, though, are secondary. Beneath them lies hurt—pain and the fear of pain.

See a child run carelessly into the street. Its distraught parent yanks it back to the sidewalk and scolds it angrily. Why angrily? Nothing happened; nothing was lost. Fear of the pain of loss, fear of what could have happened triggered that anger. In a marriage also, anger and resentment are born of either being hurt or the fear of being hurt.

Sally's first step toward resolving her resentment of Steve and his callous treatment of their abortion was understanding her hurt and pain. Only by this process was she able to eventually forgive him and begin restoring their intimate relationship. It wasn't easy for Sally. Your resolution of your unique situations won't be easy either. It takes time and involves pain, but it is essential to your survival and your marriage.

The bugaboo here is that anger and resentment quench intimacy. If you fear being hurt by this person, you cannot feel comfortable being close to this person. The fear and anger may not even have anything to do with the spouse.

One of our patients told us; "My mom was sick a lot while I was growing up. She couldn't care well for her children or participate in their raising the way most mothers did. I got tired of Mom being ill. I came to resent it and got angry. In my marriage, when my wife was ill, I found myself minimizing her illness and getting angry about it. It was a holdover from my youth, unresolved anger, something I had to work through."

We can build another formula from this:

unresolved anger = bitterness

Put another way:

anger turned sour = bitterness

Bitterness quickly and coldly quenches love and intimacy. The final fruit is hatred.

Every married couple must, therefore, master the ability to forgive. It's a skill that must be practiced daily, for husband and wife are constantly exposed to little hurts and major problems.

Anger does not just damage the marriage bond. It also damages the person. Physical problems commonly attend unforgiveness. We won't go into forty pages of medical explanation here, but put simply and basically, anger and resentment work damage in five areas.

1. They suppress the immune system.

Angry persons are more prone to bacterial and viral infections. The immune system is closely and exquisitely attuned to the body's chemistry. Chemical cues alert the immune system, so to speak, and trigger immune responses. Anything altering body chemistry therefore alters the immune system, usually in negative ways, and the specific chemical changes induced by anger reduce natural resistance to disease.

2. They alter neurotransmitters in the brain.

Neurotransmitters are chemicals that help the nerves pass information among themselves. When certain of these brain substances decrease, depression results. When they increase we see what can be called a manic condition. Altering certain others causes psychotic reactions and sometimes obsessive worry. The effects vary in different people, but they're there. In summary, anything altering these naturally produced substances profoundly affects the emotions. And when the emotions are shifted chemically, people cannot just talk themselves out of a mood. They're locked into it until the chemistry is adjusted back to normal.

3. They affect the autonomic nervous system.

This system regulates many of the body's life sustaining functions and maintains key internal balances. This system extends to every part of the body and is acutely sensitive to stress; thus, every part of the body is affected when the system overloads. Something, somewhere, eventually gives. Colitis is one of the common results, for example.

4. They are linked to heart disease.

You've heard of the Type A personality. This is the person quick to anger, time oriented, on the go. Statistically, Type A's suffer more cardiac problems and die younger.

5. They affect the hormone system.

Your hypothalamus is a tiny gland at the base of your brain connected to another tiny gland, your pituitary gland. The hypothalamus controls your pituitary which in turn controls all the hormones your other endocrine glands produce. Get the hypothalamus out of whack and secondary endocrine and hormonal disorders result. Anger affects the hypothalamus.

Most medical practitioners agree that in our modern society, up to 50 percent of physical disorders are significantly if not primarily stress related. Anger, resentment, and fear are powerful stressors. But what is most important, they can be reduced or eliminated through forgiveness.

We recommend the book *Worry-Free Living* (Nashville, TN: Thomas Nelson, 1989) by Dr. Frank Minirth, Dr. Paul Meier, and Don Hawkins for a more detailed discussion of the effects of anger and other stressors.

The Sources of Anger

"Where does your anger come from?" we ask each couple we counsel. "What is its source?"

"From him!" she always insists.

"From her!" he always responds.

It is amazing how often those answers are false. The truth lies hidden, covered by layers of denial and ignorance.

The In-laws

"Yeah!" laughs Jerry Karris. "You bet. Big source of friction." Jerry may be right, but he's not right in the way he thinks he is.

"Julia worked a long time dealing with her family-of-origin issues," we told Jerry. "How about you?"

"Some. Yeah."

"And you found out there were some serious lacks in your childhood; things you needed that didn't happen as you were growing up."

"For sure."

"So, in the dream-quest for perfect parents, you thought your in-laws, Mr. and Mrs. Marsh, would be all the things your own parents were not. And when the Marshes fell short, you projected all that loss onto them."

"Naa. I don't think so."

We weren't asking Jerry; we were telling him. But we didn't say that. Instead, we worked with him until he himself realized that was what he had done.

Anyone not dealing with family-of-origin issues (that is, unfinished business, lack of nurturing, and such) is going to have in-law trouble. If there are issues between your mom and dad, you might just transfer those issues, thinking your brand-new parents will make up for all you lacked in the past. This is a big reason there are so many in-law jokes. Ninety percent of it is projection. Jerry's problem was not his in-laws, but his denial, projecting problems with his parents onto the luckless Marshes.

It works the other way, too. In-laws who didn't resolve their own issues often transfer them onto the kids. How do you know it's happening? If you suffer chronic, constant anger, resentment, and tension with your in-laws, rest assured projection is involved.

The Irritations of Life

When you stub your toe on the coffee table and accidentally break the breakfast egg onto the burner and that acrid smoke curls up and . . . well, you have no one to blame but yourself. And that is exactly whom you should forgive. Forgiving oneself is just as important as forgiving others.

Hidden Agendas

Intense sources of anger can be volatile, hidden agendas. You may have to dig deep to find them. What anger in your life might you possibly trace to hidden agendas and family-of-origin habits?

Your Spouse

Person + person = conflict. Unavoidable.

The Expected Response

Expected by whom? By God. When Peter asked how many times one ought forgive, Jesus answered, seventy times seven, meaning in the vernacular of that day not so much four hundred and ninety times as an endless number of times. Even taken literally, we're talking daily forgiveness here. That whole passage, Matthew 18:21–35, is most instructive regarding God's attitude toward forgiveness.

What Forgiveness Is and Is Not

Julia Karris wagged her head. "No. Even if I did forgive, I couldn't forget."

" 'Forgive and forget' may be a catchword," we reply, "but forgiving is not forgetting. Forgiveness does not mean no memories. It means we choose not to go through life bitter." You can accept the offender's mistakes, choose to forgive, and still find yourself talking about what happened.

Nor should forgiveness be instantaneous. Somehow, the forgiver has the idea that once forgiveness has occurred, all those angry, hurt feelings will melt away. Then the forgiver feels guilty, for that very rarely happens. Forgiveness is not a once-and-done bandage over the wound.

You are commanded to forgive. That means you are not supposed to wait for your feelings. It's a considered decision. It is not a single act but a process. Compare forgiveness with salvation. You come to know, which is a cognitive decision with or without emotions. As you learn more, it then becomes a felt thing. Ultimately, it becomes part of you. This is a part of what Paul talks about when he urges us to the renewal of our mind in Romans 12:2.

Forgiving, however, is easier said than done.

How to Forgive

"How to forgive? Easy," said Jerry Karris. "You stand in the person's face and say 'I forgive you.' "

Would that it were so simple. Strong, healthful, effective forgiveness requires six steps.

First, Acknowledge and Admit Your Hurts

"That's quick to do," said Jerry. "Julia's always on my case for something. And her lovemaking's sort of mechanical, you know. Our marriage is on a downhill skid, and she's not trying to make it good again."

"Very well. List all the items—every annoyance and error. Write it in the form of a letter, if you wish, although your mate may not know about it. Articulate your feelings and thoughts. Some of our clients tape record the letter or dictate it. The whole idea is to help identify the hurt and pain in life. When you have a clear picture of exactly what should be forgiven, grieve the pain they caused, then burn the letter, the paper."

"You're kidding! Burn the paper? Don't show it to her?"

"That will come later. You're taking inventory of what has not yet been forgiven."

"Yes, but burn it?"

"Look at what you've done to God, and He forgave you. Our debt to God is infinitely greater than anything your spouse could do. Your bill to God is paid."

"Well, yeah, but . . ."

The six of us are all firmly convinced, based on our faith and our experience, that only a solid relationship with God provides the freedom to forgive. Put differently, no true forgiveness occurs without a relationship with God, because apart from God there is no real understanding of forgiveness.

"Forgiveness," says the skeptic, "is a divine absurdity."

The skeptic is right.

Now's a good time to examine these questions:

What has hurt you lately? (For example, *my spouse did almost nothing to celebrate my birthday.*) _____

_____

_____

_____

What severe hurts do you remember from the past (not just in the marriage but before as well)? (For example, *my dad never took time off from work to attend my childhood birthday parties.*)

_____

_____

_____

Keep these two lists firmly in mind and apply them to the steps that follow.

Second, Commit to Forgiveness

"If I weren't committed to it, I wouldn't try," you insist.

"We mean, settling in for the long haul," we reply.

Forgiveness doesn't erase the past or the effects of the past. Forgiveness must be maintained against the intrusions of the past, and that requires commitment.

Also, you cannot focus on your feelings or you'll never forgive. You can't wait to feel better about it or to somehow feel forgiving, because with every hour you wait, bitterness is festering.

Randi and James Russell came out of conservative church backgrounds; both knew from childhood that premarital sex is sinful. But they were young and in love, and this was today. Everyone's doing it today; so did they. Unfortunately, years into their marriage, Randi still had not forgiven James for coercing her into premarital sexual activity. Her smoldering resentment ate into their intimacy, into their sexual enjoyment, into the delicate fabric of their marriage. We could counsel Randi in how to forgive, using these six steps. We could encourage her to grieve the losses her resentment caused. But she had to commit to obeying Christ's wishes regarding forgiveness that lasts. In the process, both Randi and James had to take responsibility for that premarital sex.

What steps do you have to take in order to make this honest commitment?

Third, Be Prepared to Yield

And again we say, forgiving does not mean forgetting. But it does mean yielding up your right to retribution, and that is not an easy thing to do. When you are hurt, you want to lash back. Remember how Alan carried that tendency from his parents (his mom) into his arguments with Beth Anne.

How hard it is to deliberately choose not to demand that

right! Moreover, it's not something you do grudgingly. You must voluntarily turn over to God your rights of retaliation, your right to recourse. "Vengeance is mine," says the Lord. In part, that's because He's so much better at it than you could ever hope to be.

We are not talking here about legal actions and contexts. For your own health and peace of mind you must forgive your ex-spouse; it's what God wants of you. But that does not mean you excuse that ex-spouse from child support or other appropriate legal obligations. The crime victim is called upon to forgive the criminal but certainly not by withdrawing testimony or charges, which would stymie justice.

You see, at the bottom of it, the very end, all this is intended for the forgiver's benefit, not the offender's. Whether or not you consciously relinquish rights of vengeance and retribution does not depend on the sinner's state of mind. He or she may or may not seem repentant. He/she may not feel sorry or even admit to the transgression. Forgiveness is *your* thing, the action taken on *your* part. Their actions and reactions are up to them.

One more thing you must give up as a function of forgiving: "I relinquish my bitterness that you did this to me." That, too, is terribly hard to do. But it's necessary. When you deliberately put the bitterness aside, you put the issue to rest.

List ways you can accomplish this step. Be specific. (For example, *for the last year, I've withheld going to the lake for our weekend outings as retribution. Now, I choose to renew my commitment to going to the lake again.*) _____

_____

_____

_____

_____

_____

Fourth, Be Open to Relationship

Because forgiveness erases nothing, it is so often hard to warm up again to the person who wronged you. Forgiveness definitely means choosing not to carry a grudge, but you must still work through the memories. Remember that the memories live in both partners. You must have time to work through your own attitudes, and you must give the person you've forgiven time and space to work through his or her hurts also.

Two years into his marriage, Jeff cheated on his wife, Joyce, with a brief fling. With difficulty, Joyce forgave him. But in a sense she held a grudge against Jeff for coming back into the marriage after so painful a transgression. Jeff had been dealing with his conscience for several months before Joyce discovered what he'd done. He had that much time to process the pain and forgive himself. Joyce was starting from day one. She needed several months longer to deal with the issue; Jeff could not expect her to be where he was in the process.

Joyce, though, could not leave it alone. Although she technically forgave Jeff, she kept punishing him by constantly bringing it up, making sure he knew he wasn't trusted, making snide comments. Here was Jeff, a better husband than he had ever been before and determined to be faithful and loving, and she was treating him worse than she had ever treated him before. She was no longer open to an intimate relationship with him, regardless of what she claimed her feelings were.

It takes a minimum of three months, and usually six months or longer, for persons in a ruptured marriage such as Jeff and Joyce's to get over the emotional pain enough to restore the sexual bond. Even then the pain is not put behind completely. That's just the start of their return to intimacy and trusting. The person who had the affair must be patient.

There is one important exception to being open to the relationship—when one or the other spouse is blatantly abusive. We never recommend a person return to an abusive relationship until the abuser is well enough on the road to recovery that the person's health and safety are assured.

Write by name the persons responsible for the hurts you listed above. Whether their part in the hurt was intentional or unintentional, how do you plan specifically to complete this step (if one or more have died, you're going to have to get creative here)? (For example, *my wife, Jane, consistently overspent on our budget and I felt hurt by that. I'm now willing to reopen a joint checking account and work as a team on a budget.*) _____

_____

_____

_____

_____

_____

Did the steps you listed here include confessing your feelings and confronting the person concerned? That's the next step.

Fifth, Confess and Confront

Do this only if it feels right for the situation. Randi and James, whom we discussed before, had marital problems because of premarital sex. They needed to air their feelings and mutual accusations. For others there may be times when it is just not possible to talk to the person face to face. They may be separated geographically or so alienated there's not a chance the injured person could ever get them aside. Also, certain subjects should not be aired freely.

As a rule of thumb, we recommend that if there are persons whom you've dated, been serious about, perhaps have been very serious about, these are not relationships to discuss with the spouse.

Emotional struggles with such relationships are not good topics, either. Share those with a counselor, trusted friend —what some would call a confessor. When spouse A learns of B's emotional entanglement with someone, curiosity runs wild. Spouse A hungers to know all the gory details. Spouse A simply has to know what that other person looks like, where they live, what their shortcomings are. Satisfying such curiosity is not an adequate reason to discuss and argue a subject.

Spouses entangled in a dangerous emotional situation or full-blown affair must work through it. They must confess their sin against God and against their spouse. They must talk about their continued love for their mate. They must grieve giving up the outside relationship. But not with the spouse. The only time an emotionally confused or misdirected person would mention these matters to the spouse would be if that person could somehow minister to the spouse or be in some way beneficial. That is almost never the case. A possible instance would be if the spouse suspects something much worse than the actual instance. Perhaps the spouse is reading into evidence some indiscretion that is not really there.

Assume for the moment this is one of those rare cases where benefit would accrue from confession. "How do I tell her?" he asks. We advocate writing a letter and then either reading or giving the letter to your spouse. A letter can be worked and reworked until it's exactly what you want to say. You can write down—and rewrite—precisely what you want. But when you talk, the focus almost always gets shifted. You lose your point or get off on something else. With a letter there is less chance of miscommunication.

Give your person that letter when the person doesn't have to be defensive, can read it in a nonthreatening atmosphere, has no need to respond back immediately. Let the person have all the time needed to reread it, study it, think about it.

This sort of confession obviously involves confrontation. What should you do if your mate denies the source of anger or refuses to talk about it? That happens so much. What do you do?

Let's go back to the case of Randi and James and pretend that James absolutely denied that anything was wrong. He categorically refused to consider Randi's anger and resentment. "Just a hysterical woman looking for an excuse to be grouchy," he'd say and brush it off.

Randi's first step would be acknowledging her anger, to herself as much as anyone. She would write a letter telling about it. She'd pour her heart out (and almost always when a person does this, that person is shocked by the stabbing intensity of his or her feelings). Then she'd rewrite the letter into something James could read. She would explain how her anger was eating at her. She would tell how she wanted to restore their relationship to one of love and enjoyment.

Now, understand that because forgiveness is based not on the other person's responses but upon one's own needs, Randi would not have had to write those letters in order to forgive. She could have forgiven him already, without all that.

Whether James responded or not, Randi would have done her part by forgiving him. She was sincere in her efforts. If James still failed to acknowledge a problem, it would become his problem, not hers.

At times it's impossible to talk to the offender because that person is dead or out of contact. Perhaps you are divorced and didn't work through forgiveness with your ex(s) until now. You're carrying unresolved anger. That anger affects how open you are to intimacy with others. Unresolved issues—and anger is only one of many—close a person off to other intimacy. When contact is impossible, it especially behooves you to sit down and work through the issues by recognizing your anger, grieving the losses, and forgiving. (In order to grieve your loss, you may have to go to your spouse's grave or pick up a photograph of your ex-spouse and say aloud everything he or she ever did to hurt you—talk about how you felt in the relationship.)

Sixth, Put It Behind

We talked about forgiving and forgetting being two different things. You've forgiven. Now, if possible, forget. If that's not possible, don't blame yourself. Scripture says that God literally forgets our sins and transgressions once we've sought out His forgiveness. But there are only two verities in the world: there is a God, and you are not Him. Human beings, being human, cannot always erase memories. However, if you can, by all means do.

List three specific things or self-talk you can give yourself that will lead to completion of this step. (For example, you may say to yourself: a) *I've done all I can do in human power to grieve the hurt; b) God will be the ultimate judge of that other person's behavior; c) holding on to the resentment does unnecessary damage to me.*) _____
_____
_____
_____

Barriers to Forgiving

"This guy must have been coming down the escalator at a dead run," Julia Karris recalled. "One minute the escalator's clear and the next moment he's slamming into me. Bowled me over, knocked me down the two steps. I'm just lucky no loose clothing caught in the teeth of the stair as it folded up and went under. He was so apologetic. He said he was trying to catch his wife before she left the store—something like that—and wasn't watching where he was going."

"You forgave him?"

"Sure. I've done stuff like that plenty of times. I understood. Forgiving him wasn't difficult at all."

"Perhaps," we suggested, "forgiving was easy because he was a total stranger."

Julia stared at our wall a couple of minutes. "That's true. I never thought of that. If it had been Jerry who knocked me down like that I still wouldn't be speaking to him."

It's So Hard to Forgive the Individual

The people we're most likely to be bitter with, the people who most need to be forgiven, are those closest to us—husband, wife, parents. These are the persons we most need to forgive, for if we don't, we can't hope to work through the passages of marriage. And yet, they are the persons, of all people in the world, we find hardest to honestly forgive.

Julia saw her own weakness in that stranger and recognized that she quite as easily could have been the one knocking someone else down. Had it been Jerry, she would only have condemned his carelessness. There's a clue here, you see: If you can remember that no one is perfect—not your mate, not your parents, certainly not yourself—you will enjoy greater freedom to forgive.

There is, however, one person even more difficult to forgive than spouses or parents, the person closest to you—yourself. In this case, your self-talk gets in the way. You become angry with yourself, castigating yourself about how stupid you are, what others must think about you. If you are typical of people we know and counsel (and we ourselves), you are much harder on yourself than you would be on someone else. You wouldn't talk to another person the way you self-talk. You certainly wouldn't think that aloud to your best friend. Watch, therefore, for lack of forgiveness toward yourself. Talk to yourself as you would to a treasured friend, forgive your own mistakes, and move on.

"I'm not really what you'd call a women's libber," said Julia, "but there was this mechanic at a garage downtown who really got to me. I never saw him before, but here he is calling me 'hon' and 'sweetie' and laying his hand on my arm. It wasn't flirtatious; it was irritating. I told him, 'You are not my sweetie,' and he got mad instantly, as if it were my fault. Told me to get out. I was so angry, I did."

"Have you forgiven him?"

"That creep? Are you kidding? If anything, I'll call up the owner or manager and tell them why they lost my business."

"That's beside the point. Remember? You don't forgive others as a favor to them. You forgive them to heal yourself."

Forgiving others. When the others are contrite, it's easy to do. When they're hostile or unresponsive, most people don't think it's worth the trouble. And yet, forgiveness must come here as elsewhere. For Julia's sake she must forgive.

The problem is compounded when molestation, rape, injury, perhaps even killing, are the transgressions. An employee or employer, an aunt or uncle, was mean to you. You must work it through, going down the steps of forgiveness, talking through your feelings with another person or talking aloud to an empty chair (imagining the person to be in that chair) or to a photograph of the offender.

And then there's God. When have you forgiven God lately?

"Now you really are kidding!" Julia exclaimed. "God is perfect. He doesn't do anything to be forgiven for."

"True in theory," we reply, "but the heart doesn't deal in theories."

In reality, persons often hold a grudge against God because, being human, they lack the intelligence and foresight to understand why God did a particular thing. It seems so useless, so senseless, so damaging. Why did so-and-so die, or I get sick, or that tragedy come to pass? Try as you might, you can see only a tiny smattering of what He has in mind. This is a poor comparison, because God is so far above us, but think how often a small child cannot perceive what you do or feel because he simply doesn't have the ability to understand.

In forgiving God, then, we end up not forgiving Him for His shortcomings but for ours. Again, forgiveness benefits the forgiver infinitely more than the offender. If you feel a need to forgive God His inscrutibility, by all means do so.

Our Own Attitudes

"Right," Jerry pouted. "Like I'm supposed to forgive Julia for all her nagging and coldness, and then she'll turn right around and do it again."

There are all sorts of ways in which one's own attitudes bar forgiveness, and Jerry gave voice to one of them. You fear that person will just do it again. Know what? You're probably right. You are forgiving the person as Jesus commanded, and you must be prepared to forgive over and over again.

Remember the case of Jeff, who cheated on Joyce with a fling. In Joyce's case, legitimate anger lingered, and that's not all bad. God hates sin. He's angry at sin. He hates adultery. But He steadfastly loves the sinner. We must too. As we forgive the sinner we take comfort in the fact that we cannot forgive the sin. Only God can. And that must happen directly between God and the sinner. We do our part; God and sinner do theirs. The statement "I never can forgive that act" is right on.

Because you are forgiving the person, not the act, this statement does not bear weight: "I can't condone an act like that. Forgiving means putting my stamp of approval on an unforgivable act. It makes that person look all right, and he/she is *not* all right!"

Do you see the difference between condoning a possibly unforgivable act, perhaps a heinous, damaging, vicious act, and forgiving the person? Do you see the difference between the sin and the sinner? That is the difference you must make as you forgive and forgive again.

It takes strength and humility to relinquish the right of retribution and to expose our own hurt. Too much hate gets in the way. Frankly, true, complete forgiveness is not possible in human strength. We have learned from long experience that you cannot wait for the hurt to subside; you cannot wait until a feeling of forgiveness nudges into your heart and mind. It never will. The hurt will fester.

You must accept God's help by asking for His help. Call on His strength added to yours. And don't wait for a nice warm feeling. Attitudes are adjustable. At any given moment, with help from the Holy Spirit, a person can say "God, I want to initiate a spirit of forgiveness, now." And it does not depend on the other person.

Hidden agendas enter here also, shaping our attitudes without our realizing it. Therein lies the key to how you do it now. You may have to change your attitudes and methods if forgiveness in your family of origin was inadequate.

How About You?

Look into your own past, into your childhood. How was forgiveness practiced and carried out in your family of origin?

Who was expected to ask for forgiveness for transgressions in your family?

_____ Father only as head of the house?
_____ Mother only?
_____ Only children who did something wrong—never grown-ups?

_____ Whoever did the deed that needed to be forgiven?

_____ Whoever was supposed to do the forgiving?

_____ Any of the above?

_____ Nobody. Forgiveness was never a thing we thought about.

Now answer the following questions (true or false):

In our family, we were required to forget about an accident or transgression, at least on the surface, once it was forgiven. _____

In our family we never talked about forgiveness or what it means to forgive. _____

In my family I heard this phrase at least once: "I can never forgive (whoever) for (some transgression)." _____

In my family we talked about issues that required forgiveness and tried to resolve them. _____

Finally, based on what you see in your family of origin, identify two things or patterns you want to see continue in your own family, and identify at least two things you ought to change.

Two patterns of forgiveness I liked in my family of origin:

   1. _____

   2. _____

Two things about forgiveness in my family of origin I would like to change in my new adult family:

   1. _____

   2. _____

Don't worry if you can't complete all four of these statements. These blanks merely get you thinking how you can treat forgiveness in your present family situation.

"In many families," Brian Newman states, "After blow-ups, everyone drifts off. Then they return slowly into good graces again until the next blow-up. 'I'm talking to you again,' means 'I forgive you.' But the forgiveness isn't actually done or spoken. Putting it behind is not forgiving, per se. Calming down is not dealing with it. You must be willing to go back, address, and resolve the issues, or they'll just keep reappearing."

"Persons with low expectations and passive personalities tend to adjust to the dominant person in the family," Debi explains. "The dominant one is usually the most selfish. When the dominant one does something wrong, the more passive members are expected to forgive and forget without mentioning it. We see this especially in dynamics between parents and children but also between dominant and passive spouses.

"What's sauce for the goose is sauce for gander; the trick is to recognize what's happening. Both the dominant and the passive personalities must seek forgiveness. Probably what attracted these two to each other was the unchangeable characters. We're not saying to put aside dominance or passivity here. We're saying both persons must change somewhat, move closer to the center of this polarity teeter-totter."

False Forgiving

"Stuffing problems and frictions away without dealing with them is meting out false forgiveness. The issues are not brought out, the forgiveness is never spoken."

False, too, is the temptation to say "I forgive you" as cheap words to get the argument ended or to gloss over painful or difficult issues. Those simple words must be said with meaning for forgiveness to be real.

Often in counsel we see codependents attempt false forgiveness. Afraid they'll be rejected if they rock the boat, they'll say anything, then stuff their true feelings inside. You can stuff just so many feelings into a pained heart before something explodes. Stored emotions become bitterness. They will come out as passive aggression, as depression, as anxiety, as physical symptoms. True forgiveness requires that you acknowledge the pain that person's act has caused your heart, but in so doing you commence the healing process.

We often find false forgiveness cropping up in this First Passage. The relationship is not fully in place, and both persons lack the security of knowing each other well. In this passage, too, both are convinced that if we're truly in love, we shouldn't have to forgive anything. Oh, we shouldn't have conflicts! Without fully realizing it, we sweep everything under the carpet.

On the contrary, true love is *constantly* being able to say you're sorry.

Results of Forgiving

Loren and Gayle had been married two years, and they fought constantly. Sometimes she'd walk out. Usually they simply resolved the conflicts by ceasing fighting, often upon the urging of well-meaning friends who wanted to see them stay together. What they were actually doing was putting the issues aside. The issues, you see, were still available, ready to resurface at any time. Loren and Gayle's fighting lost or gained intensity from time to time, but it was always there. Nothing they fought over was resolved. They never examined the issues, and they never ever forgave.

Did Loren and Gayle have a satisfying marriage? They thought so. They didn't like the fighting, but what can you do? Their differences were irreconcilable, and you know what irreconcilable differences can lead to.

Relief came, eventually, when their friends finally got them into counseling. We helped them acknowledge that they were never resolving anything. Putting a fight aside is not dealing with it. In Loren and Gayle's case, healing commenced when they brought the issues out, examined the past to see where they originated, and then forgave each other the hurt and irritation. For six months thereafter, they would drop notes or call, telling in glowing terms about the latest forward step into further intimacy.

An issue forgiven is an issue at rest. The anger may not be resolved and certainly not forgotten. But the issue itself will not be brought up again, having been literally laid aside. Dennis Raney, counselor and lecturer on family health, and others call the stuff you drag out later "bazookas in the closet."

Unresolved anger damages intimacy; forgiveness mends it.

Without forgiveness you will get stuck in a passage. When people mature and change (and when a marriage matures and changes), they inadvertently step on each other's toes. Moreover, married people make mistakes which require forgiveness, sometimes in megadoses. Until the mistakes and issues of one passage are resolved, the couple cannot move on to the greater intimacy and new horizons the next passage introduces.

But there's far more. Forgiveness offers freedom from guilt, resentment, hostility, and bitterness. Forgiveness also means you quit trying to change or control the other person. "I will never allow another person to ruin my life by hating them," said George Washington Carver.

By forgiving, you allow God's love to shine before your spouse. But there's even more.

We cannot have intimacy with God except that He forgave us and thereby broke away the wall of sin between us and Him. Jesus in the fifth chapter of Matthew instructs His followers to leave their gift to God on the altar if they have a point of friction with another. He says to go to that person and deal with the problem; only then is the believer prepared to give a gift to God. By forgiving, you do your part toward laying the problem or point of friction to rest.

You thereby prepare yourself to freely enjoy a close relationship with your Lord.

What greater reward can there be?

Progression

Working through anger and resentment by embracing forgiveness paves the way to future growth and happiness. Now let's continue with the final tasks of this passage.

Chapter 7

Are You Making Responsible Choices?

*F*rank Minirth sits back in his chair and shakes his head sadly. "I'm dealing with a case right now. The husband is divorcing. He has a wonderful family with three kids, a good wife. He's leaving all that because he found someone else. He's back in that First Passage again, searching for romantic, idealistic love. He never made it past New Love.

"In my office this man goes on and on about what's wrong with his wife. He's projecting his own frustrations and shortcomings, you see. I can't imagine him completing the First Passage and making it into the Second with his new love, either."

How can Dr. Minirth, or any other trusted adviser, help in this situation? "First, talk simply as a friend," Frank says. "Be a listening ear. Show genuine interest. Then slowly, carefully, try to chip through his defenses, an item at a time. We all have defenses so that we don't have to see things as they are. Begin to challenge him, help him gain insight. He doesn't want to see the real picture, so an adviser must work carefully."

Frank knows how to work with that man in a clinical

counsel setting, carefully, methodically peeling away layers of denial. You the reader probably do not have such training or experience. But you can sharpen your listening. Were this man your friend, dropping that bombshell, you can listen. You can advise without judging, listen without condoning, by choosing your words carefully and saying as little as possible. Counseling is not so much advising as listening, then reflecting the person's thoughts back to him. He says; then you say, "I hear you saying . . ."

For a fanciful example, take the following script:

He: "I can't take Rose's nagging anymore. I'm going away with Gloria. Oh, I'll support my children, of course. It's my wife I'm leaving."

You (nod sagely): "I understand. The children aren't at fault. It's Rose. So you're leaving Rose for Gloria." A pause. "Gonna sell the boat, I suppose."

He: "No. Of course not. I love taking that boat out weekends."

You: "Oh. You're going to support two households, put the kids through school, and not see any drop at all in your life-style. I can't see you getting through the next fiscal year without selling the boat. You're lucky though. You have some reserves to fall back on. Like when your daughter Meghan needs braces on her teeth, you can downsize your stereo system. Probably get close to two thousand for your existing system. If you replace it with, say, a three-speaker system for eight hundred, you got twelve hundred right there. Only have to make up about three thousand more. Say, you hardly ever drive that little roadster anymore, do you?"

He: "Now wait a minute!"

You: "Meghan's got your buck teeth. So's Timmy. That's a lot of orthodontia when you're supporting two households. Even if you're not. Just trying to help."

As Dr. Minirth's client clearly illustrates, completing the First Passage isn't just a feel-good-if-you-do-it option. Fail to complete it, and disaster lurks in the wings, ready to grab center stage.

It's not too flattering a picture, but imagine this client as a squirrel clambering about in a tree. Its claws scratching in the bark, it scampers up the main trunk. Soon the squirrel has two options: climb out on this first major limb or continue up toward the other limbs. Should the squirrel move out onto that bottom limb, a large part of the tree is out of reach, for it can't get to the rest of the tree from here. The squirrel makes a choice between this branch and the next.

Frank's client has come to a major fork in his decision tree. People who care can encourage him to make the choices that will lead toward fuller branches and happier times. They can warn him away from the dead-end branches, but he may not let himself see the dead ends. In counsel we can point out what we see about the branches. With this book we hope to show you some of them and where they lead. In the end though, he, and you, make the choices.

The Fourth Task: To Make Responsible Choices

It helps the squirrel considerably to know in advance where the various branches can lead. Every decision tree is unique to the person moving through it, but all such trees share some dead-end branches in common. Dr. Hemfelt uses the tree allusion frequently in counsel to help patients recognize and make sound choices. Consider some of these branches and deadwood in relation to your own marriage. We'll make them very general so you can interpret them according to your situation.

The Urge to Run vs. Hanging Tough

A number of fears hit newlyweds between the eyes during the first few years of marriage: "What's the big deal about intimacy? You say that this or that leads to greater intimacy as if intimacy were a goal. Not to me, it's not. I want my space, and my wife can keep hers. Too much intimacy messes up a relationship."

That's fear talking. To be intimate is to be vulnerable. Many people, men and women alike, are afraid of that kind of vulnerability. Other fears are just as common. For instance the young married sometimes thinks: I'm stuck. I just bought into one sexual partner for a lifetime. I wonder what would have happened if I had married someone else? Would they have been better?

Fear of entrapment turns up frequently as we talk to clients. Such fears bring divorce or abandonment to the minds of most newly marrieds sooner or later. Bailing out is definitely a dead-end branch, but in the face of fear it may well look inviting. This includes threatening to bail out too ("That's it. No more. I'm going home to Mother.").

As Dr. Hemfelt points out, the urge to run has never been easier to indulge than in the twentieth century. "There are few—if any—moral, social, or even ethical stigmas attached to divorce. We've lost the powerful peer pressures that used to keep people married. We're even losing the economic pressure to keep people married."

Bolt or stay? These are the two major choices, and there is no undoing the damage if you take the wrong fork.

Resisting Change vs. Going with the Flow

Here is a major limb on the choices tree that pops up frequently in marriage: to adjust and compromise or to resist change and pretend things are working.

A case in point: Gretchen and Tim Heusen. Gretchen and Tim both grew up in fairly affluent families. Eight months into their marriage, they were begging Daddy Heusen and Daddy Mullins to help them get their credit cards under control and cosign for their house. Wisely, daddies Heusen and Mullins conferred together before addressing the newlyweds and discovered the problem.

The daddies knew that newlyweds almost always take a big drop in their standard of living, and logically so. Their earning power is nowhere near where it will be someday; their assets are negligible because they've not had time to accumulate. Gretchen and Tim, however, chose to pretend their circumstances had not changed. They could not adjust to the new reality and, as a result, had acquired heavy debts beyond their ability to pay.

Their story has a happy ending, though not an easy one. Daddies Heusen and Mullins sat down together with the kids, showed them how to consolidate debts, and offered advice on how to live more economically (both dads knew a trick or two in that department; both had started with nothing). The couple were smart enough to listen to their fathers' counsel. Six months later, when Gretchen and Tim showed they were adjusting to the new reality by making good progress at paying off their debts, their dads bought the house themselves. Today, they rent it to the kids as an income property. When Gretchen and Tim have built up enough savings for a down payment, they'll be able to buy it.

This is a case where the squirrel started out along one branch, realized it was the wrong one, and turned back to make a different choice. The Heusens were able to adjust their life-style expectations.

A lot of couples are not so wise. In our times, most people try to start their marriage at the same economic level as their parents, when it took their parents years to obtain that financial status. Susan Hemfelt's parents began with just a card table and boxes for furniture. Today's newly marrieds can't conceive of doing this.

For instance, Mark Brown was a CPA, making $25,000 to $28,000 a year. Jessica, his wife, came from a wealthy family. The first year of their marriage, she went wild with the charge cards, going to the department store every chance she got. She was still living within her daddy's life-style. They both wound up in counsel when their finances were a disaster and all communication had broken down.

"Didn't you both sit down and plan a budget?" we asked Mark alone.

"Sure. But Jes just looked at the budget. She wouldn't stick to it—still buying everything in sight."

Jessica Brown had not adjusted to her new life-style. Her expectations remained high even on Mark's moderate salary. Their story also has a happy ending. Although Mark was up to his ears in debt from Jessica's spending habits, he didn't want a divorce. They could begin to adjust their expectations of each other and their life-style.

Selective Perception vs. the Real You

Mary Alice Minirth talks about another aspect of adjusting. "Throughout our marriage, Frank and I have been careful to keep time apart for each other. It's not easy. A lot of times we've had to improvise—to be flexible. For instance, during his years of internship and getting started in practice, the kids and I would go over to the hospital to eat supper with him. It was the only break he had at a reasonable hour. Today, we may go out for breakfast before he does his radio show. Spur-of-the-moment things like that keep the romance alive and well. You have to roll with the punches; you have to be ready to improvise."

A third way newly marrieds will find themselves at this fork is when the new starts to wear off. People in courtship try to keep their best foot forward. Still somewhat uncertain about their relationship, newlyweds maintain their best behavior, just as they did in courtship. That stuff never lasts. Both partners must be ready to adjust to the surprises as the real spouse emerges bit by bit.

Consider again the case of Mark and Jessica Brown. Jessica fondly envisioned Mark as a breadwinner making any amount she needed. After all, Daddy did. Mark assumed he had married a lady like Mom, who knew the value of a dollar and spent frugally. The attitudes, of course, arose in courtship. Remember selective perception back in courtship? Each was seeing only what they wanted of the other, not reality.

After time passed in the marriage, their facades wore off. Mark and Jessica began to see the true person in each other —a rude awakening. Their challenge now was to adjust to living with these new and sometimes disappointing personalities.

It wasn't easy, which is why most couples bail out at this point. Those who remain find enormous freedom when they no longer have to keep up this front to attract their mates. They can now truly be themselves, and in doing so, they are loved by their spouses. In the best of circumstances, this love matures. The move from fantasy to reality is so crucial that we will explore it as the first task in the next passage of marriage.

How About You?

Remember in Chapter 3, we discussed the need for unconditional acceptance of each other? When the flush of courtship and new love fades, unconditional love is needed more than ever. Even though unattainable in the pure sense, it is worth every effort. As our true selves are unveiled, we need our mate's acceptance and love. And we need to reciprocate with the same feelings and support.

What adjustments did, or does, your particular situation require?

Write them out below. (For example, *I know I am too rigid in demanding that everything in our household be in place and be orderly. I need to let go in that arena.*)

1. _____
2. _____

3. _____

4. _____

5. _____

How comfortable are you about adapting to them?

The last task of this First Passage of Marriage deals with the passages of marriage themselves. Sooner or later, you and your spouse must recognize your parents' incomplete passages or they will join those other ghosts that can haunt your relationship.

The Fifth Task: To Deal with Your Parents'
Incomplete Passages

We have some good news and some bad news for you. The bad news: All the unresolved issues of the prior generations, those time-release beads that have been accumulating down through the years, are visited upon you. These time-release beads are different from the family patterns we've discussed in former chapters; those were simply attitudes or methods of family life. These issues can be very destructive to your relationship. Yet they often lie so deeply buried beneath your conscious mind that you cannot tell they are there. You cannot escape them either.

The good news: Although others failed to work out these issues in the past, usually because they didn't realize they were there, you can go back and untangle them. Recognizing the issues foisted upon you by prior generations is half the battle. Over and over, our patients and clients tell us how very liberating it feels as they see what is happening in their lives.

The prior generations leave many kinds of unfinished business for our generation and our children's to mop up— or suffer with. Not all unfinished business consists of incomplete marital passages. Unfinished business is anything the parents started and did not complete—dreams they entertained but did not fulfill; elements of life such as the opposite sex or fractured personal relationships with which they never made peace. However, *all incomplete passages become unfinished business for the next generation.*

The next generation must complete the unfinished business or it will plague the generation to come. If you are the next generation, you condemn your children either to complete or to suffer with the unfinished business you do not handle now. There is no easy way out.

These "ghosts" from your family of origin will haunt your marriage throughout its passages. For this reason, dealing with the multigenerational issues will be a task of most passages. That past—our forebears, our childhood, our family of origin, our previous traumas—is sometimes expressed in a set of symbolic statements. As we step up to the altar to speak our "I do's" before God and the world, our hearts speak one or more of these other "I do's" nonverbally.

1. "I DO attribute to you, my new partner, all of the unresolved negative gender stereotypes propagated by my mother and father." Lucky you.

By *propagated* we mean set forth by the parents. Grandparents, aunts, and uncles qualify here too. Negative stereotypes, such as "No man can be trusted; they'll all stray on you," "Women have no skill at managing money," and "Men can't be expected to have sensitive feelings," may all spill over into the marriage.

We recall one couple in their First Passage who, during courtship, were absolutely eloquent in their words of endearment, commitment, and affection. Shortly after the honeymoon, the wife began to notice that, although her husband still displayed interest and affection, he never said "I love you." Gone were the impassioned declarations. When she drew it from him in a passive way: "Do you love me?" he could say yes. There it ended.

In the rural region where he grew up, men didn't express affection. That wasn't manly. His dad took it a step further. He delighted in teasing Mom and would never say words of affection in front of the kids. The only way Dad related to Mom in front of the kids was derogatory. "How's the old bag today?" Obviously, husbands cannot be tender or endearing.

Interestingly, the woman came to the hospital for tests. She suffered vaginal pain with no discernible physical cause. Doctors referred her for counseling. She was hurt and angry that her supposedly loving husband would not speak his love. The vaginal pain became an expression of her anger and hurt. Once both of them figured out what the problem was, the dysfunction was resolved. Now he knows it's okay to be tender and endearing in marriage as well as in courtship. And when he starts to slip into the old stereotypes, she's quick to put him back on track.

2. *"I DO set about to continue the battle of the sexes unresolved between Mom and Dad. I do carry the banner for Mom or Dad by reenacting the unfinished battle."*

"I see, now," said another patient we'll call Jerry. "If I had married a love-kitten, instead of Stone-Cold Molly, I wouldn't have been able to keep up the fight." The unresolved battle of the sexes between Mom and Dad continued clear through Jerry's extended family. Aunts and uncles, cousins, siblings all harbored resentments and hostilities against the opposite sex. "It all started back with that women's liberation thing," Grandpa grumped. "Things were okay till then." No, things weren't. Jerry had inherited a battle generations old.

Because Dad had a long-standing war to force Mom into sexual compliance and performance, Jerry unconsciously picked a frigid spouse. Jerry and his wife had two new battles to win. Jerry had to recognize that this battle was Dad's all along and hand it back to him; Jerry had to make new decisions for himself. The second battle was his wife's.

She had shut down internally. Now she had to go back and explore why.

We suggest that you think about the fights between your parents. Be wary of that old nemesis of denial, the natural response that causes us to minimize painful things in order to survive in a family. Also realize that often we literally can't see the forest for the trees. Everything about our family is familiar. It is family to us. Therefore, we don't tend to see the fallacies in our parents' relationship. And be aware of those time-release capsules lying in wait.

Recent clients of Brian and Debi Newman had such a capsule that colored their early conflicts. Debi explains, "Each time Kevin and Joan Davenport had an argument, Joan would leave the scene and lie down on the bed in their spare room. For her, it was a chance to cool off, to get away from the emotions of the moment. Kevin, on the other hand, acted very threatened."

Brian explains, "When Kevin's mother and father had a disagreement, his mom left the room and retired to the guest room. It was the same when Kevin and his mom had an argument. That meant case closed, no more discussion. The issue was never brought up again. Mom got her way by withdrawing from the conflict. But it never got resolved."

Counselors and therapists call this passive aggression. By not doing anything or operating with subtle innuendos, the person is achieving what they want. In essence, they are winning by lying down, a common and very effective weapon. We normally think of aggressive people as violent, strong, dominant. But an aggressive person can be just as dominant if they act quiet and meek. Adding to the power this action represented was the fact that Kevin's mother was ill a lot in his childhood and many times convalesced in the spare bedroom.

Brian continues, "When Joan did this, Kevin felt that same despair. He felt threatened by her actions. He was back again in his mom's house, never winning an argument and helpless to change it."

"Joan didn't realize how much her actions affected Kevin," Debi says. "When we explored the issue with them both, Joan saw how upset Kevin was when she went to the spare room, just like his mother did.

"The problem was Joan had a legitimate need to withdraw from the incident and cool off so she could think clearly. It was her method that was threatening. We talked them through the conflict-resolution process. Through lots of understanding and patience, Kevin has come to accept Joan's need to cool off and leave the situation for a while. But he was only able to do this when she proved to him she was committed to resolving the issue. Joan did that by agreeing to meet with Kevin at a later time (specific time and place) to discuss the problem. And she had to follow through several times to convince him."

Brian smiles as he remembers the case. "Joan also had to make her actions less threatening to Kevin, avoiding the trigger for his time-release capsule. Now, she tries not to use the spare bedroom as a place to cool off."

3. *"I DO seek a safety zone in this marriage by selecting a spouse who will not challenge or threaten the area of greatest apparent vulnerability in my parents' marriage."*

The power of this "I do" is so great that the person may overselect, making an extremely "safe pick." For example, the daughter of an authoritarian, tyrannical father chose a totally lifeless, passive wimp as a safe pick for marriage. Everyone who met him said, "Huh? Why?" The reason, of course: That partner would not run roughshod over her life. She found, six months into her marriage, that he didn't even run smoothshod over her life. He didn't run at all. Within months she was bored mindless with the guy, left without a spark of romance or sensuality. "It's like being married to a potted plant."

Uncovering the Real Issues

Often the battle of the sexes will be fought on battlefronts that involve authority issues, financial matters, sexual intimacy, and time sharing. Look carefully at the bottom-line cause of friction between your parents. To help patients identify these issues we often suggest that they look at their parents' relationship in five different ways.

The Known Conflict

For instance, you might have heard Mom complain over and over again that Dad doesn't make enough money or Dad doesn't know how to manage the money he does make. That's the overt conflict. Think about the arguments between your parents and determine the known conflict:

"When my mom and dad argued, it was most frequently about _____.
They also argued about _____."

The Suspected Conflict

You may have never heard either of your parents talk about this issue or fight about it, but you have a hunch that this problem was there, just below the surface.

Or this suspected conflict may be an underlying layer of the main conflict. For instance Mom might have continually complained that Dad was a poor breadwinner, but in reality Mom was a compulsive shopper. Dad never confronted her about it, so the real conflict between them was hidden.

"I suspect that an underlying conflict between my parents was _____."

Underlying Fears

Behind all conflict and all anger is fear. We always ask patients if their parents had any strong fears. For instance,

Mom never acknowledged her fear of poverty, but she did talk about the Christmas her only gifts were an orange and an apple and a new pair of shoes because her father was out of work during the Great Depression. Her underlying fear was "We will never have enough to avoid some financial disaster. We are going to run out of money and lose all we do have."

"I suspect that my mom's underlying fear was _____."

"I suspect that my dad's underlying fear was _____."

Disappointments or Disillusionments

Now ask yourself, *Did either of my parents experience any great disappointments or disillusionments?*

For instance Mom may never have said so directly, but you came to realize that she didn't see your father as "Mr. Right." This doubles the ante for you, if you're a girl, as you try to find "Mr. Right." It also doubles the ante for your husband to always perform as "Mr. Right."

"I suspect that my mom has been disappointed or disillusioned by _____."

"I suspect that my dad has been disappointed or disillusioned by _____."

Finally, we suggest that you compare notes with other family members.

Input from the Extended Family

Sisters or brothers, aunts or uncles, grandparents are your extended family. When we counsel patients, we often ask permission to talk to a relative in a special session or by telephone. The phenomenon in family relationships can be illustrated by that old story of five blindfolded people who tried to describe an elephant. One touched the tail and described a hairy ball; another held the ears and described long floppy wings; another felt the tusks and described a hard cylinder. Each person had a piece of the picture, but no one could give a complete description of that elephant. We all see our family of origin with that same narrow perspective.

We suggest that you fill in the missing pieces by talking to someone in your family. Play back the memories of your parents' disagreements together. Then think about their actions. Any signs of war? It's yours as well as your parents' unless you give it back to them.

Concerning Jerry's wife (alias Stone-Cold Molly), incidentally, she eventually found out she harbored massive guilt and anger about an abortion forced on her by her parents. She thought she had put all that behind her, but stuffing it away is not grieving it through. She still occasionally goes back to grieve what her parents did to her and her unborn child.

How About You?

Give these three "I do's" a lot of thought. Discuss them with your spouse, and then listen to what each other says.

What is your conclusion about their effect, if any, on your union?

_____

_____

_____

_____

_____

_____

And if at any time you feel you are in over your head, that you have uncovered something too big and too ugly to handle, do seek professional help.

Each of these choices will affect your marriage in this passage and in others and stunt your opportunity to grow. Only commitment to each other and to the marriage makes growth possible.

Chapter 8

Are You Committed and Have You Completed the First Passage?

S omehow, it seemed that every time Carl and Alan ended up in the same place at the same time, so many other things were going on, they had no time to chat. Today, for once, they could sit and talk. Carl hefted his coffee mug. "More?"

"No, thanks. I, uh, have a question. It's, uh, rather personal."

"Shoot."

"We learned in college that when a marriage partner dies, the survivor tends to romanticize the relationship. He or she paints the picture of the past much rosier than it actually was. I know that Beth Anne and I think everything is terribly romantic. It's a lot of fun. Now I'm scared it's going to wear off. It didn't seem to wear off for you two, though. Beth Anne and Annie both say you and Bess have been perpetual newlyweds your whole marriage. How did you manage?"

Perpetual newlyweds? "Hardly." Carl shook his head. "I know for sure, if you leave a marriage to its own devices, you'll drift apart."

"Experts agree with that. So how do you avoid drifting apart?"

Carl pondered the question a few minutes. He sipped his coffee; it was stone cold. "You start out pretty naive. You commit yourself to marriage not knowing what the blazes you're getting into. No matter what you think it's gonna be—no matter what your dreams are—it turns out to be something different. I guess . . . I guess, you commit yourself to go with the flow, whatever the flow ends up being."

"Commitment to stick with it."

Carl nodded. "And commitment to stick with it *together;* I mean really together. Not just to stay undivorced but to stay truly married." A thought struck him suddenly. "You don't marry a dream or a way of life, you marry a person. The dream might change, the way of life probably will, and the person certainly will. And so will you. We all do. Your commitment is to that person all the while you're both changing."

Alan frowned. "You mean you consciously adapt to each other?"

"I doubt you do it consciously, at least not much. Bess and I got off the track a couple of times. Found ourselves drifting away. The conscious part is seeing what's happening and taking steps to bring yourselves back together.

"You're gonna grow, regardless. So when you see yourself growing apart, sit down and figure out how to grow together."

Nurturing Growth in Your Marriage

There are a number of ways to maintain the momentum of growth, and thereby complete the passages. These suggestions are not intended to be a rote list. We offer them as a beginning, a guide to help you think how you might nurture growth in your specific situation.

Commit to Union of Purpose and Action

"Let not the left hand know what the right is doing" may be a good almsgiving policy, but it's sure no way to run a marriage. Commit yourselves to make no important decisions without consulting one another. Questions of finance, child-raising, life-style, major purchases—all pertain to the marriage partners as a unit, not as individuals, for the welfare of the marriage itself depends upon harmony in these (and other!) areas. You are working as a team now; teamwork requires that the members keep in step, each knowing what the other thinks and does.

This is not the surface example sometimes given of wifey getting hubby's approval to buy a new vacuum cleaner. This is husband seeking the wife's counsel, as she does his. Two heads are indeed better than one.

Sharing decision making benefits the marriage, but the very process of making decisions jointly provides a far more important by-product—improved intimacy. As two persons work out complex issues, each learns more about the other —how that person thinks, what matters to that person, what that person needs at the deepest level.

We often suggest that couples consider another essential area of growth in their marriage—spiritual growth, which unites their marriage to the purposes and values of the God of the universe, who first ordained marriage.

Commit to Spiritual Growth

Persons completing this First Passage must trust that God exists beyond their family of origin. "Nonsense!" you fume. "Everyone knows that!" Sure they do, intellectually. But in childhood the heart has other ideas, and those ideas must be put away. The heart and head are often miles apart.

The family of origin provides the original source of security. The spiritual challenge of this First Passage is to rip those deep taproots of security out of the family of origin and plant them in the new union.

Too, Mom and Dad were surrogates for God. In a sense, they were God. Now they must be lifted from that pedestal.

We urge you also to combat the youthful tendency toward extremes. At one end there is agnosticism: Is there a God and do I need Him? This doubting, healthy in itself, may be covert. If you've grown up in a strongly religious home, you may feel guilty about doubting or failing to evidence perfect faith. Questioning and doubting are natural among Christian couples. As they hustle to develop a firm union, a career or two, a family, a life, they tend to lose sight of God's role in their lives.

The other extreme is a blind, unthinking, unowned allegiance to the God of your family of origin. What do you believe? Why do you believe it? Is your faith your own or a cop-out in which you let your family of origin make these decisions for you?

The same couple may vacillate between the two extremes. When agnosticism becomes threatening or frightening or unfulfilling, the couple reverts to the family-of-origin spiritualism, comforting and rote. Back and forth, back and forth. Neither position is the couple's own.

The newly marrieds cannot know God as profoundly as can older people, but they can separate Him from the past and bring Him into the present and future of their new life together. Prayer to that end avails much. So do study and the inner examination of values. The new attitude toward God is an individual walk, of course, but develop it also as a couple. Study together. Pray together. Find fellowship together with believers of like mind. Explore God and His claims together. Identify God with your new family in every arena of your spiritual life.

Commit to Lovemaking

Now that the First Passage is coming to completion, we need to restate the commitment to lovemaking we discussed in Chapter 5. Society and the media give far too much emphasis to the role of sex as recreation or amusement and far too little to its power to unite man and woman at the deepest emotional level. It is no accident of nature that newlyweds, bathed in the euphoria of Stage One New Love, instinctively make maximum use of this bonding tool. Lovemaking is an important part of building intimacy.

Commit to Romance

Again, at the risk of repeating ourselves, romance is so critical, you must recommit yourself to keeping it alive as you leave this passage. Remember the excitement and spontaneity of this powerful tool. Keep it vibrant as you grow older together—a kiss or hug unsolicited. The same for the declaration "I love you." Give a small gift or flowers (for the male also). Take leisurely walks, holding hands as you did in courtship and early marriage years. Go on an occasional honeymoon, away from the kids, the jobs, the house, just the two of you talking and spending time together as lovers.

The Newlywed Game

Beth Anne and Alan shifted uncomfortably on the Naugahyde sofa. Bright sunshine streamed in the basement window of Pastor Ron's office. Alan fidgeted with his shirt collar. Beth Anne squeezed his hand and smiled.

"This isn't an inquisition you know," Pastor Ron reassured them. "I like to touch base with my couples every now and then. You gave me the opportunity when you asked me to renew your marriage vows. Seems to me you both just celebrated an anniversary. Is that right?"

"Two years," Beth Anne said. She squeezed Alan's hand again.

"Congratulations. Now, before we go further, would you like to play a little game?"

"I guess so," Alan answered. "How about you, Beth?"

"Sure, why not?" Beth Anne agreed.

"Okay." Pastor Ron grinned and pulled out a manila folder from his desk drawer. "Ever see 'The Newlywed Game' on television?"

"Lots of times when I was growing up," Beth Anne answered. "They asked couples all kinds of dopey questions. It was pretty funny—the way a player answered when their husband or wife wasn't there."

"What about you, Alan? Ever see the show?"

"Not really. I didn't watch much television when I was growing up. I heard about it, though—some game that showed how little married folks knew about each other."

"Right. Most of the couples had been married less than one year. The show was very entertaining. But it also represented a good marital exercise. How would you like to play a newlywed game now just for fun?" he asked.

"Might be interesting," Beth Anne said. She glanced at Alan and giggled.

"What's so funny?" Alan asked his wife.

"Oh, I was just thinking about some strange quirks of yours that I didn't know existed until I married you."

"Like what?" he asked.

"You know," she answered, giving him a knowing look.

Alan flushed deep red. Pastor Ron chuckled. "I'm not asking for intimate details. Alan, why don't you use my desk. Beth Anne, you can stay on the couch. I'm going up to the balcony to talk with the organist. I'll be back in a few minutes."

He paused at the door, "Oh, by the way, the game will be more fun if you stick to the rules."

"What rules?" Alan asked.

"Just like on television, answer the questions without talking to each other. Otherwise you'll be cheating." And then he was gone.

Beth Anne looked at the first question. *Let's see Alan's favorite color is, ummmm, black. That's all I ever see him wear; must be. And my favorite color is red, always has been.* She pulled down her red sweater and continued.

Alan's favorite song, boy that's a toughie. What's that one about thunder and lightning by Garth Brooks? I'll put that down. Mine's "The Rose" by Bette Midler. Wonder if Alan knows that?

Over at Pastor Ron's desk, Alan struggled. He thought, *I don't know any of these answers for Beth Anne. I'll just fill them in for myself and skip down. Here's one I know: If I really want to make Beth Anne mad, I'll bring up the dinner party we had with her college roommate. Boy, was she furious. I guess I was rude, but Beth Anne's friend bored me silly. Her date was no better, spouting off politics and such. My horse would have been better company.* He smiled and scribbled his answer.

Sometime later Pastor Ron stuck his head in the door, "How're we doing?"

"Fine, all finished." Beth Anne said.

Alan looked sheepish. "I've done as much as I can."

"Great." Pastor Ron sat down across from both of them.

"Want to share the answers?"

Alan looked dubious.

"Why not?" Beth Anne said.

The results of this little exercise showed Beth Anne and Alan that they had come to know each other well in some ways and not at all in others. Beth Anne had a good handle on Alan's superficial likes and dislikes. Yes, his favorite color was black. But she didn't know much about some of Alan's more serious attributes. Alan, on the other hand, hadn't paid much attention to Beth Anne's surface characteristics—he had no idea what was her favorite color or song. But he sure knew what things impacted her the most. He was right on the money with the dinner party incident.

How About You?

Take time to answer the following newlywed questions. As Alan and Beth Anne did, fill in the answers separately and then discuss them together. See how well you've come to know this person you've lived with for the past two years or so.

My spouse's favorite color is _____

(My favorite color is _____)

My mate's favorite song is _____

(My favorite song is _____)

The place we were when my partner first knew he/she was in love _____

(The place I was when I first knew I was in love _____)

My spouse will say his/her favorite part of my body is _

_____

(My favorite part of my spouse's body is _____)

If I really want to make my partner mad I will bring up _____

(If my partner really wants to make me mad, he/she will bring up _____)

The famous person my mate would most like to meet is _____

(The famous person I would most like to meet is _____ _____)

My spouse's most cherished possession is _____

(My most cherished possession is _____)

The Task List

"Now that we've had some fun and you've learned a little more about each other, let's find out about the third party in this arrangement—your marriage," Pastor Ron continued.

"What do you mean?" Alan asked. He had been reluctant to come with Beth Anne to this counseling appointment. After all, they had gone through premarital counseling. Then Beth Anne came up with this hair-brained scheme to renew their vows. He had agreed mainly to please her. But he had to admit that this discussion was interesting.

"One of the things I like to do with a couple is show them how far they've progressed since the wedding. We try to emphasize the positive accomplishments and point out where adjustments might be needed to improve things a bit. Any issues caught now will be that many less to tackle later.

"I'm going to give you this set of statements to fill out if you wish," Pastor Ron explained. "They are grouped according to tasks that a couple should strive to complete at about your stage of marriage."

He handed one copy to Beth Anne and another to Alan.

"Looks like a test," Beth Anne remarked.

"Yeah, right out of Sociology," Alan agreed.

"Don't worry about these questions. They aren't meant to scare you. What I'd like each of you to do is to go through them and simply check whether they apply to you or not. Each statement measures how much you and your marriage have grown over these past two years.

"Also, this little exercise is for your benefit as a couple. Once you've each filled them out, I want you to discuss them together and see where you may need to make any adjustments in your relationship. As a matter of fact, you don't have to share any of the answers with me. Work on them as a couple. If you find an area where you're stuck, you can ask me for guidance. Sound all right?"

"You mean we don't have to turn this in?" Beth Anne

asked. "It's a take-home quiz that we don't even have to do?"

"Not unless you want to."

"Now that's my kind of test," Alan said.

"And mine too," Pastor Ron responded. "Let's briefly go over these to see if you understand the statements." He started reading down the list:

"Task 1—Mold into one family. What do you think that means?"

"I dunno," Beth Anne answered. "Does it have to do with our leaving our parents and 'cleaving' to each other, as the Bible says?"

"Close," Pastor Ron answered. "This task measures whether you each have successfully uprooted from your parents' home and have formed a new home together. Each of the statements gauges how well you've done."

"Do we also have to fill these out separately and then talk about them together?" Alan asked.

"That might be helpful," Pastor Ron answered.

Alan shifted his position. He was enjoying this session. Looking over the statements, he could see some definite points he wanted to talk over with Beth Anne—like the fact that she wouldn't ever let them spend a holiday without her parents or grandparents. It's not that he didn't like her relatives—he really enjoyed her grandfather. It's just that he wanted a chance to have one holiday alone with her. He'd looked forward to taking her on a morning horse-back ride this past Easter with the church youth group. But, noooo! Her mother had a brunch planned.

"Task 2—Overcome the tendency to jockey for control. That's fairly obvious. My wife and I still struggle with this one after nearly thirty years of marriage," Pastor Ron commented. "I'll bet you both have had to make lots of accommodations on this score."

"Yeah, I'll say," Beth Anne replied. Alan looked at her in surprise.

"Ooops," she said. "Well . . . you know how it can be."

"Yes, I do," Pastor Ron smiled. "Again, check those statements that apply to you. The number of statements you've checked will alert you to how well you've handled conflict so far. And, let me tell you, this will be immensely valuable the longer you're married.

"Task 3—Build a sexual union. I'm not going to go into detail on these with you. Check these statements if they reflect your current sexual relationship. I just want to remind you both how important a sexual union is to your marriage." Pastor Ron looked at both of them to emphasize his point.

Beth Anne squirmed a little. Alan pulled at his collar.

"Task 4—Make responsible choices. What does that mean to you, Alan?"

"Glad you asked that," Alan said. "I just had a conversation about this very thing with Beth Anne's grandfather."

"You did?" Beth Anne interrupted. "When?"

"Last Saturday morning, while you went shopping with your mom. Committing to the marriage through purpose and action."

"Well put," Pastor Ron replied. "These statements reflect how well you've made certain decisions together, for instance with finances. They measure how committed you are to working together as a team."

"Looks obvious enough," Beth Anne commented as she perused the statements under Task 4.

"Good. And, the final task. Task 5—Deal with your parents' incomplete marriage passages. This will take some explaining." Pastor Ron looked at his watch. "If we still want to renew your vows, we won't have time to do this subject justice. How about if we make another appointment to talk about this?"

"Fine with me," Alan responded.

"Me too," Beth Anne agreed.

We will pick up Alan and Beth Anne's discussion of Task 5 with their pastor in the next chapter. For now, though, let's see how well you think you've survived Passage One.

Now It's Your Turn

How well has your marriage survived this First Passage? Is the passage completed? Take the time to participate in this same exercise with your husband or wife. Make a copy of this inventory so you and your spouse can take it individually. Check the statements below that apply to you. Ask your mate to check those that apply to him/her without consulting you. That's cheating. Don't worry if you or your spouse can't fill in all the blanks.

Now come back together to talk about your results. This is the type of inventory we make when we determine if a couple has completed the First Passage. We invite you to make your own assessment and make any adjustments that seem possible to improve your relationship. The statements are grouped under the specific task.

Task 1—Mold into One Family

1. _____ When I use the word *home,* I am referring to my spouse's and my place of residence.
2. _____ When I have good news, the first person I think to tell is my partner.
3. _____ I always ask my mate's advice on important decisions.
4. _____ My spouse and I sit down together at our kitchen or dining room table to eat a meal together at least three times a week.
5. _____ I have spent at least one holiday this year alone with my husband/wife.
6. _____ I regularly attend some sort of worship with my spouse.

7. _____ There are some issues concerning my mate and I that I do not discuss with my family of origin.

8. _____ My partner and I share a time of spiritual meditation alone at least two times a month.

9. _____ When I'm sick, I count on my spouse to take care of me.

10. _____ I can imagine living even thousands of miles away from my parents.

11. _____ I am willing to bend on issues that have popped up regarding the nitty-gritty of married life: who balances the checkbook, who does what cooking, who scrubs the toilet. As evidence of this, I can cite the following example: _____

Task 2—Overcome the Tendency to Jockey for Control

1. _____ I don't try to win arguments with my spouse, but I try to understand my spouse's point of view during conflict.

2. _____ I have made as many sacrifices as my partner when it comes to decisions about our life together.

3. _____ I have been willing to give in to my mate on at least one issue that was important to me.

4. _____ I feel secure in my spouse's love for me.

5. _____ The overall attitude in our marriage is one of sharing.

6. _____ I don't force my mate to go places or spend money he/she doesn't want to or be with people he/she doesn't want to be with.

7. _____ I value my spouse's opinion as much as I do my own.

8. _____ I don't feel a need to know what my partner is doing every moment of the day.

9. _____ I don't call him/her more than once or twice a day while we are apart.

10. _____ My goal is not to change my spouse.

11. _____ My partner does not complain that I am always telling him/her what to do.

12. _____ We agree on who should balance the checkbook.

13. _____ We agree on how often to visit family.
14. _____ We have reached agreement, or at least an armi-
stice, on some major control issues. Two specific
instances I can point to that demonstrate progress
are:
1. _____
2. _____

Task 3—Build a Sexual Union

1. _____ I feel comfortable with the frequency of sex.
2. _____ I feel comfortable talking to my spouse about sexual
issues.
3. _____ Sexual intimacy is very important to me.
4. _____ If my mate made me feel uncomfortable sexually, I
could tell him/her.
5. _____ I don't pretend to have an orgasm when I don't have
one.
6. _____ I like to come up with new ways to keep our sexual
intimacy exciting.
7. _____ When I think of our sexual intimacy, I think positive
thoughts.
8. _____ I don't find our sexual intimacy painful.
9. _____ I have experienced sexual times that were somewhat disappointing.
10. _____ I enjoy our sexual intimacy.
11. _____ I can honestly claim that our sex life is open and
honest and enjoyable for both of us, more so than
in the beginning. A way in which it is improving
is: _____
12. _____ I am willing to open up into intimacy. One recent
instance in which I let myself be vulnerable to my
mate is: _____
13. _____ Okay. So I am willing to admit that my romance
with a perfect partner is an illusion. As evidence
that this statement is true, I offer the following incident or point: _____
14. _____ I am willing to pursue romance with my spouse
anyway. Three instances lately in which my partner

and I made a romantic gesture or pursued some romantic fantasy are:

1. _____

2. _____

3. _____

15. In this last week, my spouse and I found time alone together (other than in bed) _____ times.

Task 4—Make Responsible Choices

1. _____ I am aware of the bills my spouse and I owe.

2. _____ I discuss major decisions with my spouse.

3. _____ My mate and I never purchase anything over a certain amount of money without consulting each other. That amount is: $ _____

4. _____ My partner and I have a family budget.

5. _____ I don't do things behind my spouse's back.

6. _____ I realize that the decisions I make affect my mate as well as myself.

7. _____ I don't seriously consider divorce as an option to our marital problems.

8. _____ I understand that it's important for my partner and I to agree on when to have children.

9. _____ I feel accountable to my mate for the decisions I make.

10. _____ I am willing to say no to something that is important to me to make time for my spouse.

Renewing Vows

"Alan, do you again take Beth Anne to be your lawfully wedded wife? To have and to hold her no matter what shall come?"

"I do," Alan answered. He looked into Beth Anne's eyes. The love he saw in their depths brought tears to his own. *I love you more than the day we were married,* he said to her with his eyes.

"Do you, Beth Anne, again take Alan to be your lawfully

wedded husband? To have and to hold him no matter what shall come?"

"I do," Beth Anne answered. She gazed into Alan's eyes. She felt faint, as if she and Alan were alone and surrounded by a circle of filmy light, bathed in love. Even more than her wedding day, she felt she was doing the right thing in the eyes of God. "Thank you, Lord, for giving me him," she murmured softly.

"I now repronounce you husband and wife. You may kiss each other," Pastor Ron proclaimed.

Quite a while later, he cleared his throat.

"Ohh!" Beth Anne exclaimed. She blushed.

Pastor Ron smiled. He placed his hands on their heads. "Let us pray."

Outside on the steps of the chapel, Beth Anne and Alan thanked Pastor Ron for his time. "It was my pleasure," he answered. He turned to go back in the church. "Oh, by the way, have you decided to make it binding?"

"Pardon?" Beth Anne asked.

"Have you prepared a marriage contract?"

"No," Alan said. "Should we do that too?"

"Glad you asked," Pastor Ron turned and walked back toward them. "Let's do it."

Chapter 9

Writing a Marriage Contract

*M*any counselors urge their clients—indeed, everyone—to keep a journal of thoughts and feelings. This journaling serves two purposes. It helps the person articulate feelings more clearly and therefore see what those feelings are. And it cleanses (called catharsis, technically) by releasing pent-up feelings and unspoken thoughts. Writing a marriage contract does much the same job as journaling.

Beth Anne and Alan, like many couples, never prepared a marriage contract. And those couples who do enact a contract do one primarily for financial reasons—to safeguard one or the other in case of a breakup. By contrast, the marriage contract we're speaking of safeguards the couple *from* breakup.

Preparing a marriage contract, or revising an existing one, provides a guide and beacon for the passage to come. As you lay down the contract guidelines, you can see where your marriage is heading. Even better, you can guide to a large degree the way it will go. You can launch into the next passage with aplomb, confident that intimacy will grow in healthy ways.

"Yes, but a marriage contract?" Alan wrinkled his nose.

Most people sneer, not realizing how valuable such a contract can be. You might want to do this exercise over the next few weeks.

Here are some guidelines to help you write, or rewrite, a contract for your own union. In prior chapters we asked you to identify contract elements, for example in financial and sexual matters. You will want to include that here. But there is much more.

The Groundwork: Task 5

There are several things to do before a couple sits down to write the actual contract. One of these is to explore possible causes of time-release capsules *before* they go off. Forewarned is forearmed.

Beth Anne and Alan chose a weekend getaway to start their groundwork. The Sunday paper littered the hotel room floor. Beth Anne placed their breakfast dishes outside the door.

"How about now?" she asked.

"How about now what?" Alan asked. He grinned and hugged his wife.

"You know, work on this contract thing."

"Now?"

"Well that's what we wanted to do this weekend, isn't it?"

"Yeah, you're right. Okay, let's do it."

They both sat down at the small table by the window. Alan flipped through the pages in front of him. "This looks like a lot of work."

"We've already done some of it when we filled out the questionnaire Pastor Ron gave us. I even brought it along." She fished it out of her duffle bag.

"Always prepared. Get that from your mother." Beth Anne shot him a blistering look. "Ooops. Time-release capsule again. Sorry. But I meant it as a compliment." He squeezed her shoulder.

"The first item is to inventory our parents' marriage. We did that under the Task 5 questions. Do you remember the discussion we had with Pastor Ron on this issue?"

"Do I ever!" Alan answered. "I had no idea this stuff could be so serious." And, he remembered the talk they had with Pastor Ron . . .

"Now, the final task: Task Five—Deal with your parents' incomplete marriage passages. Have a clue what that's about?" Pastor Ron had asked both of them.

"Not a one," Alan answered.

"Neither do I," Beth Anne agreed.

"This is a little more difficult. Researchers have uncovered an interesting family phenomenon of intergenerational patterns. In simple terms, problems and issues your parents or even your grandparents failed to deal with in their marriages can be passed on to you for you to handle in your marriage."

"Not my folks!" Alan snorted.

"Everyone's. Some hidden agendas are benign, even helpful. Others can cause severe problems. Unresolved issues—unfinished business, they're called—can haunt you and Beth Anne in your current marriage. And, what's even more alarming, if you two don't finish the business in your marriage, the problems can be passed on to your children's marriages."

"How on earth am I supposed to solve my mom and dad's problems?" Beth Anne asked. "I wouldn't even know where to start. I don't even know if I want to."

"I'm not asking you to solve your mom and dad's problems. The gist of this task is to make sure those problems don't become yours in your relationship with Alan," Pastor Ron explained.

Alan carefully looked over the statements under this task. "I see how powerful these things can be," he commented.

"If I really want to get Beth Anne's goat all I have to say is, 'You're acting just like your mother.' "

"Exactly," Pastor Ron said. "Our parents influence more of our actions and thoughts than we realize. It's not an easy thing to pick out, let alone deal with. Terri and I constantly have to watch for these time bombs in our marriage. However, merely identifying these issues will help stop their damaging effects. Let's take an example. From what I hear, you've been in on a few horse roundups, Alan."

Alan brightened and sat up—finally, a topic right up his alley. "Ranch herds and mustang roundups both. It's a great chance to really see the potential qualities each breed has; to pit your judgment against the horse sense of the guy next to you."

"In the roundups I'm familiar with, at least two corrals are used to divide the herd."

"Yeah." Alan could almost smell the dust as he described it. "You drive the herd into a larger corral. Then horse by horse you run them into an adjoining corral. A hand on the fence has to be pretty fast to close the gate behind each horse. Otherwise, you'd have the whole herd in the next corral. It's pretty tricky when there's a stallion involved. He doesn't want to leave his harem."

"It's been a while for me." Pastor Ron admitted. "What would happen if that hand on the fence didn't ever slam the gate?"

"It'd be impossible to split the herd. You'd just be driving the horses round and round from corral to corral," Alan answered.

"Exactly. Task 5 is that gate. The horses represent all that unfinished business."

"I see," Alan said. "If we recognize these hidden issues, we can close the gate and keep them from running into our marriage. Right?"

"In theory. But I warn you, it gets harder the longer

you're married. Which is why I suggest you both tackle this subject now."

"All we have to do is elaborate on those issues." Beth Anne's comment yanked Alan from his thoughts of that past meeting with Pastor Ron. "Here, you work on your parents' and I'll work on mine." She handed Alan a piece of paper.

What About You?

Use the following list of thought-provokers to see how much your parents are influencing your current relationship. Beth Anne and Alan went through a similar checklist with their pastor.

Task Five: Deal with Your Parents' Incomplete Passages

1. I'm willing to see that my parents are not perfect. (true or false)
2. My parents' unfulfilled dreams (that I can recall) were:

   _____

   _____

   _____

3. I don't feel pressure to fulfill my parents' unfulfilled dreams. (true or false)
4. I'm not motivated to fix my parents' marriage by making my own marriage work. (true or false)
5. I recognize the influence my family and my partner's family have on us as a couple. (true or false)
6. I am willing to step out of my old family into the new one. Evidence that I am maturing into the new life as a marriage partner, or have done so, is:

   _____

   _____

7. I have not come as far out of my family as I would like to, as illustrated by this instance:

   _____

   _____

8. Three things I can do to reduce family ties are:

1. _____

2. _____

3. _____

Now that you've put your memory into action on your parents' relationship, do the following exercises with Beth Anne and Alan to channel those memories.

Inventory Your Parents' Marriage

First, ask yourself what tasks of the First Passage your mom and dad went through well and what went not-so-well. Be very specific about this. You are looking for incomplete tasks, tasks that were glossed over or avoided. Check the tasks your parents have completed.

Beth Anne began down the list. She looked at Task 1 and felt that her parents had not accomplished this very well, especially her mom. Annie Warden Millen spent much of her free time at the home of her parents.

_____ Task 1–Mold into One Family (Did either of your parents seem to rely too heavily on their parents?)

Beth Anne had a good idea how her parents dealt with control issues. Her mom, Annie, simply ran the show and her dad let her mom do it. *I must watch this tendency in my own relationship with Alan,* she thought. *I don't want to be overbearing like my mom is with my dad.*

_____ Task 2–Overcome the Tendency to Jockey for Control (Did either of your parents always try to win arguments or make all the decisions?)

Alan found that his parents had not successfully built a sexual union. In fact, they had taken to sleeping in separate bedrooms. "Your father sleeps like a noisy eggbeater," his mom had complained. Now Alan wondered if something deeper wasn't wrong.

_____ Task 3–Build a Sexual Union (Did your parents seem comfortable with their sexual relationship?)

When Alan considered Task 4, he had to admit his parents seemed to work out decision making. In spite of all the yelling and arguing, they always hashed out major issues. They worked together as a team—albeit a tenuous one.

_____ Task 4–Make Responsible Choices (Did your parents seem to make important family decisions together?)

Beth Anne couldn't answer how her parents dealt with her grandparents' incomplete passages. She thought Bess and Carl Warden had a model marriage. And she never really knew her father's parents. They both died when she was very young.

_____ Task 5–Deal with Their Parents' Incomplete Passages (Did you see any similarity between your parents' marriage and your grandparents'? You may have to pull at straws here. Search for any nagging memories. Were there any common behavioral patterns among all three relationships?)

Are There Hidden Contracts?

For this next point you will engage in a fair degree of speculation and subjective judgment. You are simply exploring. Each of you should make a list of hang-ups and hidden contracts you suspect in your parents' marriage—i.e., when your mom and dad do what they do, what might the true underlying reasons be? Work on this the way you listed lousy reasons to marry, back in courtship.

Alan listed the following things right off the top of his head about his parents:

- "Insecurity seems to be a hidden issue of my mom's. She always needs people and things around her. She was an only child. She always had material possessions but never had much love when she was growing up."

- "My dad lacks confidence. He seems to really love my mom, but he purposely acts helpless to get her attention."
- "As much as my mom complains, I think she really likes having to do things for my dad. Maybe it's a case of power. She likes the power."

Beth Anne listed the following items about her parents:

- "My mom immerses herself in activities. Maybe she's trying to escape the real, hard issues of her marriage. She might be afraid of admitting her true unhappiness with my dad. I sure felt it growing up."
- "My dad has slowly withdrawn year by year from my mom. It's like he isn't even home. Maybe he's also afraid of facing the reality of their marriage, except he's coping by escaping. I'd be surprised if he hasn't had an affair sometime in their marriage." (The mere thought of it punched her in the stomach, a sucker punch that surprised her in its viciousness.)
- "My mom always refers to how good a marriage her parents have. In fact, she spends a lot of time at their house. Always has ever since I can remember. Maybe she feels her marriage should be like her parents', and she's unhappy because it isn't."
- "I think my dad always wanted a son. When I was a child, he told me I was going to have a brother someday. Then my mom got sick and couldn't have any more children. Wonder if that explains why he never exhibits much affection toward my mom?"

Your list may be similar. Let your mind spill out its memory banks. Put down every image or thought from your childhood concerning your parents. Think of all the things they did that might point to hidden agendas and then list what those hidden agendas might be. Try to write at least five statements.

1. _____

2. _____

3. _____

4. _____

5. _____

List any subtle, stated contracts your parents observed in their marriage. You may have heard them over and over as a child. Their underlying meaning could greatly affect you in your marriage now. Check the following list where it applies to you. Then add some more of your own at the end.

_____ Mom or Dad used to say: "I only stayed with your mother (or father) for the sake of you kids."

_____ Dad or Mom said: "The only reason I stay at this lousy job is to put food on the table and a roof over our heads. If I didn't have a family to support, I'd be out doing _____."

_____ Your mom or dad frequently said, "I'm the only one who does anything around this house, your father (or mother) never does anything useful."

_____ You've heard one of your parents say: "Sex is a duty in a marriage."

_____ Your mom or dad may have said, "It's the woman's duty to stay at home and take care of her husband and children."

Beth Anne and Alan could check at least one of the above statements. How about you? Can you add some more?

_____

_____

_____

_____

Share the Information

"We're supposed to share the insights we've gleaned from this exercise about our parents," Beth Anne read. "And show each other where there might be hidden agendas at work in our current marriage. Want to go first?" she asked Alan.

Alan listed the following insights:

1. My parents were verbally abusive to each other. I have caught myself doing that to Beth Anne.

2. Some of my sexual encounters with Beth Anne have been disappointing since the wedding. I wonder if my parents' separate bedrooms have anything to do with this?

How About You?

Share everything you've learned and guessed with each other. Work on what you've found, talking about it together. Each will probably stimulate the other to better memories and insight. What hidden contracts and secret agendas might you expect in your marriage now and in the near future? Try to think of at least 3 items:

1. _____
2. _____
3. _____

Inventory Your Own Marriage

Each person should do this independently. Only later will the two of you come together and compare notes. Beth Anne and Alan decided to do this over the next couple of weeks separately. They made a date to meet and discuss their results.

What tasks have you completed well?

Go ahead. Boast!

_____ Task 1: Mold into One Family
_____ Task 2: Overcome the Tendency to Jockey for Control
_____ Task 3: Build a Sexual Union
_____ Task 4: Make Responsible Choices
_____ Task 5: Deal with Your Parents' Incomplete Passages

What tasks have you failed to complete?

_____ Task 1: Mold into One Family
_____ Task 2: Overcome the Tendency to Jockey for Control
_____ Task 3: Build a Sexual Union
_____ Task 4: Make Responsible Choices
_____ Task 5: Deal with Your Parents' Incomplete Passages

Alan and Beth Anne found they had done fairly well at becoming one family and making responsible decisions. But they needed more work on control issues, their sexual relationship, and dealing with their parents' hidden issues.

What might be some hidden contracts—time-release capsules?

Write down what you see as possible hidden agendas, either of your own or as unfinished business from your parents. Speculate. Let the mind explore freely.

Beth Anne could provide the following item that worked as a time-release capsule: "I so desperately want to be different from my mom that I react whenever anyone says 'I look or act just like my mom.' My hidden agenda might be that I am so afraid of having my life turn out like hers, I might go overboard in the opposite fashion."

Look over the following list. Check any that might apply to you and then add some more at the end.

_____ I find myself acting just like my mother (or father) in an argument with my spouse.

_____ I expect our house to be run exactly the way my mother did hers.

_____ In heated arguments, I revert to techniques my parents used in their disagreements (for example, name-calling, giving up, leaving the room).

_____ I find myself doing _____ (that I don't like) as a negative means to get my spouse's attention.

_____ I expect my spouse to be a certain way to make me happy.

_____

_____

_____

_____

What are your own "stated" (that is, declared) contracts?

The Power of the Unknown

An example of where an unspoken contract was violated was in the case of a woman in our counsel who suffered vaginismus. Her vaginal muscles spasmed down so tightly, she could not have intercourse. She came in for help; nothing like that had happened before in her marriage. Briefly, what happened was this: During their first passage of marriage, she dropped out of college and went to work to put her husband through school. The unspoken promise was, when their family was established, she would go back and finish. She was a good sport about it. Years later, the kids in high school and her husband secure, she planned to return to school. Semester after semester, her husband came up with one excuse or another as to why this was not a good time. Later. Always later. She made no conscious rebellion to his counsel; after all, it was logical. In her mind she saw no violation of that old agreement. But involuntarily, below conscious level, her heart resented the abrogation of their agreement, and her body shut down in protest. Literally.

So bring these hidden contracts out in the open and recognize them. They can be very damaging if left unspoken and undeclared.

Fill in the following list where you can. Add your own at the end.

_____ "I intend to complete my education."

_____ "I want to help you find the perfect job. I am willing to move anywhere in (this state) (this country) (the world) if that's what your work requires."

_____ "I intend to put my career on hold when we have children. But I expect you to allow me to resume my career when I am ready by giving some of yours."

_____ "I do not intend to take out the garbage. That's your job."

_____ "I am not interested in balancing the checkbook or paying the bills each month. Just let me know how much money I can spend each month."

_____

_____

_____

_____

Now come together and compare your lists. With these assessments you've done most of the beginning contract work already. The next step is to actually write out the contract. Beth Anne and Alan were anxious to get the nitty-gritty on paper.

The Actual Contract Process

After that sorting process, about what do you find you agree? Is there an impasse, a place where you're stuck, an incompletion? Now is the time to write out a contract to cover these points. In effect, the contract delineates why the two of you choose to be together.

There are two components to this contract: the broad parameters, which are the major mutual contract issues, and the give-and-get. Page 175 shows the basic ingredients of a marriage contract. Just like a good recipe, follow its general format, and improvise where needed for your particular unique relationship.

Broad Strokes

Begin with the broad, sweeping generalizations.

"I will not abandon you. I am committed to you for life."

"I want to nurture you and help you reach your best."

Your statement of commitment may not be as absolute as "I am committed for life." Perhaps in all honesty you must say, "I thought about leaving but I will not contemplate that for at least a year."

Next, be certain in this section to state some honest affirmations about each other and about the marriage.

"I admire the way you stand by me when your mother gets picky and cross."

"I really like the way we're able to do things together on the weekends."

"You have a great attitude toward charity and social responsibility. I admire you for that."

Beth Anne had this affirmation to state to Alan: "I really like the way you tolerate my impatience. Since I've been married to you, I have learned to slow down, relax and enjoy life more."

Give and Take

She explains what she needs. She tells him what she wants. He explains what he needs. He tells her what he wants. Now both declare what each is willing to give in order to get what he and she want and need. In short: "What am I willing to give in order to get?"

Rare is the couple who can agree right down the line on the same contract agenda, the same give-and-take. Agreement is not the goal. Adjustment is. You may well reach the decision that you have quite different reasons and agendas for this marriage, but you will give each other what you need.

The husband may want to carve out a vocational identity while his wife is struggling with the question, "Yes, but do you love me?" If his job is keeping him away from home fifteen hours a day, she may well wonder. Here's the place to air the differences and reach mutual understanding, if not agreement.

The give-and-take may be quite specific: "I want you home at least two nights a week."

"I want a date night once a week, just the two of us."

In this section lie the antitheses to the dysfunctions that are starting to crop up. We nurtured John and Marsha through this process in the clinic. John was to write down at least a dozen reasons why he liked women and a dozen reasons why he disliked or distrusted them. He could only come up with seven reasons why he liked them, but the dislike reasons filled a page—single-spaced.

Marsha had exactly the same problem. As the two of them started looking at this objectively, they discovered that they were using each other for sparring partners. Much of the time they were intensely angry with each other; the true object of their anger was the opposite sex.

John then wrote out specifically what he wanted in place of that hostile, dysfunctional relationship. So did Marsha. Each stated in writing that he or she was genuinely willing to commit to a peaceful, harmonious marriage. Then each very specifically declared what he or she would give up and what positive steps he or she would take to reach the goal of harmony.

How About You?

Do as John and Marsha did. List the reasons why you like the opposite sex (sex itself constitutes only one reason; sorry). List the things you hold against men in general, women in general.

Do the same for your own sex. What do you like and dislike about the fellow members of your gender?

What does this tell you about your sexual beliefs? How might those beliefs be affecting your marriage, for better or worse?

_____

_____

_____

The Plan for the Future

Each spouse writes out a new agenda and tasks. These goals might be similar for both or quite different. What one person sees as a big-ticket item may not be significant for the other. They may reflect joint effort (better financial harmony, better teamwork in parenting). They may be individual goals. She wants to take on more projects in the church and he wants better success at work.

Write down whatever it takes to move along through this passage and meet individual and mutual needs.

Both Alan and Beth Anne agreed to work harder on how their parents' hidden agendas may be influencing their own relationship. Alan wanted to delve into his sexual issues and see if his parents' unspoken positions were influencing his experience. Beth Anne wanted to watch the tendency to control as her mother does. They wrote these items out as new tasks they needed to work on.

The Goal of Any Contract

The premise, in the end, becomes: if we can meet each other's needs, and help each other with the tasks that must

The Marriage Contract

1. Statement of extent of commitment to each other and to the marriage

2. Statement of affirmation: at least one attribute each person admires and appreciates in the other

3. Statements of Give-and-Take
   a. List each person's needs for the marriage
   b. Negotiate what has to be given by each person in order for those needs to be met
   c. Write out adjustments that may be needed in the current or future relationship to accomplish the most critical needs

4. Statement of recognition of old, dysfunctional hidden agendas

5. Declaration of new agendas to redress any dysfunctions

6. Statement of tasks successfully completed from Passage One

7. Declaration of Tasks from Passage One which still need more effort by the couple together and steps needed to accomplish those tasks successfully

8. Statement of any hidden, unspoken contracts. Formalize their accomplishment (time period, steps needed)

9. Details of everyday life (request for date nights) Use items brought up under give and take

10. Statement indicating when contract should be periodically reviewed and updated (anniversaries are a good time)

be completed, we will move through the passage trium-
phantly! This is the antithesis of dysfunction.

You have to do your homework. If you haven't analyzed
your parents' marriages and dug out hidden agendas, the
surface patch-up will surely fail.

For example, in the case of John and Marsha, if they
don't root out that hidden contract—that they consider
each other sparring partners—any new contract will do
nothing more than set them up to fail. It will become a
self-fulfilling prophecy that fighting is inevitable.

Shallow marriage counseling won't work here. In fact,
most people sense that counseling won't work even when
they don't know why. The why is, they didn't do the
groundwork.

Fortunately, Alan and Beth Anne had done the groundwork, even though it wasn't easy. They were very relieved
when they had written a contract and now keep it in a
special place—next to their marriage license. And they have
promised to pull it out every so often for updating.

Digging for Deeper Intimacy

At the Minirth-Meier Clinic and in more casual settings,
we often use quizzes and inventories to help couples explore their needs and feelings together. Improved intimacy
results. Following are some thought-provokers to help you
and your mate tap the riches of the First Passage and its
grand love. Debi Newman uses these fun exercises in her
counseling and teaching sessions to help her clients clarify
their issues and feelings. Take time to enjoy these with your
spouse.

1. Anniversary Memories
Start a scrapbook or blank diary or add pages to your wedding keepsake book to record how you spend each anniversary.

2. First Anniversary Questions:
What was your happiest memory of your wedding day?

_____

_____

_____

What was your happiest memory from your honeymoon?

_____

_____

_____

What was your happiest memory in your first home together?

_____

_____

_____

What is the most surprising thing you learned about your mate this year?

_____

_____

_____

What are the five strongest areas of your marriage? (finances, sex, friends, leisure, careers, religion, time together, communication, conflict resolution, in-law issues)

1. _____

2. _____

3. _____

4. _____

5. _____

How do you hope to see your marriage grow in the next year together?

_____

_____

_____

3. Dreaming Together

This First Passage is a foundational period in your marriage. You will start out your bond as two very different people than you will be ten, twenty, and fifty years into your marriage. There will be some dreams you will keep throughout your marriage, and some will seem silly ten or twenty years from now. Yet, it is fun to dream together. Decide together on some dreams you share in the following areas. Write out these dreams as a couple:

Vacation Dreams

_____

_____

_____

Personal Dreams

_____

_____

_____

Career Dreams

_____

_____

_____

Spiritual Dreams

_____

_____

_____

Retirement Dreams

_____

_____

_____

Keep your list around and review it every five years to see

how many you have achieved and how many you don't want anymore.

4. Planning for Children

Some couples don't have time to plan for children because they marry with children already on the scene. Other couples plan to wait awhile or don't talk about it and end up pregnant unexpectedly. Some even discover well into their marriage that one partner doesn't want children at all. It's important to plan as much as you can.

How many children do we want to have? _____

When do we want to have children? _____

_____

Does our insurance cover maternity and prenatal care? _

_____

How will we care for our children? (Mom at home, Dad at home, day care, nanny in home)_____

_____

5. Setting Up Traditions

You don't have to wait until you have children to build your own family traditions. What are some traditions you can begin now as a couple? (For example, getting away at least one weekend a year [alone], establishing certain holidays to spend certain ways, giving each other meaningful gifts.) Think of at least three traditions you want to begin now.

1. _____

2. _____

3. _____

What are some traditions that we want to set up for our anniversary? What are anniversary dream vacations we would like to take at ten years, twenty-five years, thirty-five years?

1. 10-year Dream Vacation: _____

_____

2. 25-year Dream Vacation: _____

_____

3. 35-year Dream Vacation: _____

_____

6. Spending Quality Time Together

The early years for many couples are a time without children. Make sure you take advantage of this time together.

If I knew this was my last year alive, what are some important things I'd like to do? (list at least three)

1. _____
2. _____
3. _____

Who are some couples we would like to spend time with this year? (list at least two)

1. _____
2. _____

What is the best way to spend time with people? (For example: eating out, having people over, playing games, renting videos.)

1. _____
2. _____
3. _____

When Beth Anne and Alan filled in these last few blanks, Beth Anne had to compromise a little. She learned how much Alan hated formal dinner parties. The two of them had to agree on the most enjoyable means of entertaining. Now if Beth Anne wants a formal affair, she understands Alan may prefer an informal barbecue in the backyard.

What are personal goals, couple goals, other goals, that we want to achieve before we have children? (Think of at least four.)

1. _____
2. _____
3. _____
4. _____

7. Learning About Each Other

The happiest day of my life before I met you was:

_____
_____
_____

The saddest day of my life before I met you was:

_____
_____
_____

Something I never told you about me is (use discretion):

_____
_____
_____

Something I would want you to know about me is:

_____
_____
_____

My most embarrassing moment was:

_____
_____
_____

My best friend as a child was:

_____

_____

_____

My friends and I used to:

_____

_____

_____

If I could be someone else for a day I would be:

_____

_____

_____

One of the craziest thoughts I ever had was:

_____

_____

_____

I wish I had never:

_____

_____

_____

I'm really sorry I never told _____ that:

_____

_____

_____

From La-La Land to the Real World

Alan and Beth Anne were completing their First Passage of marriage. Thanks in part to the guidance of their pastor and friends, they were continuing on the road of marriage in good shape. Their marriage (their vehicle) had recently had a tune-up (the marriage contract) and was running as smooth as a top. Their road map to the future looked much like the tasks displayed on pages 186–87. Leaving this passage successfully, they had nowhere to go but forward.

At about two years of marriage, the observant couple will notice a lot of changes in the relationship, and not all the changes are good. This marks the beginning of the Second Passage of marriage.

In this Second Passage, new love gives way to reality. As in the First Passage, the couple must complete various tasks successfully to accomplish this transition, such as:

Task 1: Hang On to Love after Reality Strikes

Life is as busy and hectic now as it's ever going to get. Kids, the jobs, and the house add pressures. The couple may find themselves swept out to sea by a tide of busyness. Too, the gloss of the newlywed years has worn off. Reality has set. Any expectations dreamed of in the first two years are popped one by one in this reality stage. Statistically, the highest divorce rate hovers around this period. Temptations for extramarital affairs are particularly enticing. And sadly the priority of the marriage drops to last or a close last.

Too, as the couple jockeys for balance between each other, one takes up the slack the other lets drop. Polarization—natural in most cases, but damaging in the extreme—occurs. As one spouse becomes more dominant, the other becomes more passive. The couple must now strive to keep this polarization from being destructive.

To meet the challenges of this task, the couple must learn some hard things about themselves such as taking responsibility for their own happiness. They also must re-commit to making their marriage a high priority close to the top, even above the children and careers.

Task 2: Childproof Your Marriage

Children can be a blessing to any couple. But they also can wreak havoc on any relationship, no matter how loving and benign they may be. The equation:

$$1 \text{ person} + 1 \text{ person} = \text{conflict}$$

is now expanded to be:

$$1 \text{ person} + 1 \text{ person} + 1 \text{ person} + 1 \text{ person, and so on} = \text{conflict increased exponentially}$$

Kids provide all sorts of demands and energy drains the couple never even dreamed existed—financial, emotional and physical. Husband and wife find themselves running a marathon just to meet their family's and jobs' needs. Their marriage is left out in the cold. To survive this task, the married couple learns to childproof their marriage to restore its intimacy. By providing a happy and fulfilling marriage, they are meeting their children's primary need—family stability.

Task 3: Recognize the Hidden Contracts in Your Marriage

The time-release capsules we discussed in the First Passage are in full force during this reality phase. Both spouses must weed out and bring these hidden agendas into the open. If left uncovered until this stage, they will explode in some vicious fashion. During the first two years of marriage, the couple is still trying the water. By the Second Passage, they've dived in head first. The hidden agendas which remain underwater act like submerged rocks waiting to injure the diver.

Each partner must recognize and confront these hidden agendas before they hurt themselves or their mate or dissolve the marriage.

Task 4: Write a New Marriage Contract

The contract prepared as part of the First Passage will be no longer valid after kids, careers, and partners have changed through this Second Passage. This last task requires each partner to review and update their contract, adding any new issues and removing those that have been achieved.

As the tasks in this First Passage were challenging, so will they be in the Second Passage. The efforts to accomplish them will reward the couple with an enriching life together. You might want to read *Realistic Love,* the second book in our series on the passages of marriage, to prepare yourself for this Second Passage.

If you and your spouse feel yourselves ready to enter the Second Passage having successfully completed the First, plan a celebration—a graduation of sorts. And pat yourselves on the back.

You deserve it.

Major Tasks of All the Passages of Marriage

THE FIRST PASSAGE–NEW LOVE
(The First Two Years of Marriage)

Task 1: Mold into One Family
Task 2: Overcome the Tendency to Jockey for Control
Task 3: Build a Sexual Union
Task 4: Make Responsible Choices
Task 5: Deal with Your Parents' Incomplete Passages

THE SECOND PASSAGE–REALISTIC LOVE
(From the Second Anniversary through the Tenth)

Task 1: Hang On to Love after Reality Strikes
Task 2: Childproof Your Marriage
Task 3: Recognize the Hidden Contracts in Your Marriage
Task 4: Write a New Marriage Contract

THE THIRD PASSAGE–STEADFAST LOVE
(From the Tenth Anniversary through the Twenty-fifth)

Task 1: Maintain an Individual Identity along with the Marriage Identity
Task 2: Say the Final Good-byes
Task 3: Overcome the Now-or-Never Syndrome
Task 4: Practice True Forgiveness
Task 5: Accept the Inevitable Losses
Task 6: Help Your Adolescent Become an Individual
Task 7: Maintain an Intimate Relationship

THE FOURTH PASSAGE–RENEWING LOVE
(From the Twenty-fifth Anniversary through the
Thirty-fifth)

Task 1: Combat the Crisis of This Passage
Task 2: Reestablish Intimacy
Task 3: Grieve the Particular Losses of This Passage

THE FIFTH PASSAGE–TRANSCENDENT LOVE
(Beyond the Thirty-fifth Anniversary)

Task 1: Prepare for Retirement
Task 2: Continue Renewing Love
Task 3: Achieve a Transcendent Perspective
Task 4: Accept My One and Only God-given Life

Notes

Chapter 3
1. Jerry D. Hardin and Dianne C. Sloan, *Getting Ready for Marriage Workbook* (Nashville: Thomas Nelson, 1992), 151–154.
2. Ibid., 159–160, 162, 164.
3. Ibid., 178.
4. Ibid., 185.

Chapter 5
1. Hardin and Sloan, *Getting Ready,* 193–195.
2. Ibid., 201–207.
3. Ibid., 220–221.